Themes of the Times for Social Welfare Policy

Readings from

The New York Times

Second Edition

Edited by

Peter A. Kindle

University of Houston

ISBN 13: 978-0-205-53024-3   ISBN 10: 0-205-53024-9

10 9 8 7 6 5   11 10 09

I. PERSPECTIVES ON SOCIAL SECURITY

Social Security reform captured news headlines repeatedly as recently as 2005. Personal accounts, as explained in the first article, were touted as a superior option, yet left unanswered the question of how personal accounts would provide adequate retirement and disability assistance for the unemployed and underemployed. The second article places Social Security reform in its political context and suggests the generation gap that exists between older and younger Americans on this issue. The third article discusses Robert C. Pozen's idea of returning Social Security to financial balance without dismantling the progressive benefit structure that has been one of the programs greatest successes. Today Social Security reform may appear quiescent; however, as the last article notes, the financial projections seem bleak. In its current form Social Security is not sustainable. Reform of some kind seems inevitable.

As you read the following articles, consider how you would answer these questions.

1. Economic View: Who Wins in a New Social Security? (03/06/05)

- Who is penalized the most by raising the retirement age? Why?
- How does the preservation of the "progressive nature" of Social Security promote intergenerational conflict?

2. Republicans Weigh Voter Response to Retirement Plan (03/10/05)

- Why are older voters "especially important in off-year elections?"
- How did Bush miscalculate older American's opposition to Social Security reform?

3. A Democrat on Bush's Social Security Team (04/30/05)

- Who is most likely to benefit from Pozen's plan to bring "financial balance" to Social Security?
- Why is Pozen's "support for private accounts" described as "natural?"

4. Finances of Social Security and Medicare Deteriorate (05/02/06)

- What changes are necessary to make Social Security sustainable?
- Which program is in worse financial condition — Social Security or Medicare?

Economic View: Who Wins in a New Social Security?

By Eduardo Porter
March 6, 2005

Social Security may have done more to help the poor than any other government program in American history. Established in 1935 with the explicit objective of protecting the elderly from poverty, it has relied on a heavily skewed benefit formula that pays lower-income workers a higher share of their wages than those at the top of the earnings ladder.

The results? According to government figures, old-age poverty has dropped from about 50 percent in the 1930's to around 10 percent today. Most of the credit goes to Social Security.

Yet as President Bush sets out to reconstruct Social Security, by allowing workers to divert some of their payroll taxes into personal accounts, crucial questions remain unanswered: Would a new system retain the traditional approach of redistributing income from the more affluent to those in need? Or should personal accounts—framed by Mr. Bush as a step toward an "ownership society"—usher in a system in which workers keep what they actually save?

The president argues that workers can get a better return on their payroll taxes if they invest them themselves.

ment of social policy, using part of the taxes paid by some groups to shore up the benefits of others.

Any changes made to the system will inevitably shift this distributional mix, and that troubles some members of Congress. "Social Security is a central strand in our social safety net," said Senator Gordon H. Smith, Republican of Oregon, the chairman of the Senate Special Committee on Aging. "I believe its progressive nature has to be preserved," he said, adding that he would hold his vote "in abeyance" until "we address these progressive issues."

Social Security uses taxes from the rich to bolster the retirement income of the poor through a benefit scale that now replaces about 60 percent of preretirement earnings for low-income workers but only 30 percent for the workers in the highest earning band.

But the program has a multitude of other objectives, moving money every which way. An essential reason for the decline in old-age poverty, for example, is that older generations—which paid lower payroll taxes—have received transfers from younger generations, who have paid higher taxes to get the same or even lower levels of benefits.

survivor benefits that depend on the earnings of the working spouse. And the program's disability insurance favors workers in tougher jobs, mainly at the lower end of the income spectrum.

Social Security's income redistribution includes some unintended quirks. Survivor benefits are regressive, favoring people whose spouses were high earners. And the nation's changing demographics have created a patchwork of winners and losers that, to some extent, has overridden the system's original purpose of favoring the poor.

That's because Social Security is more generous to people who have more time to collect benefits, like women, who are expected to live three years longer than men, on average, after retirement, and whites, who, after reaching 65, are expected to live a year and a half longer than blacks.

Calculations by C. Eugene Steuerle and Adam Carasso of the Urban Institute offer this contrast: A 65-year-old single man who retires this year after a career in which he earned an average of $36,500 a year, in 2005 dollars, will get $164,000 in retirement benefits over the rest of his life, on average, based on his expected life span of 81.1 years. That is about $8,000 less than he would receive if he invested his payroll taxes at a 2 percent rate of return, after inflation.

But a single woman with a similar earnings profile can expect to receive $206,000—or $28,000 more than she would get by investing the contributions at the same 2 percent rate, merely because she is likely to live longer.

Because the poor and the less educated tend to have lower life expectancies, they sometimes end up getting a worse return on their payroll taxes. According to projections by Mr. Steuerle,

> *And the nation's changing demographics have created a patchwork of winners and losers that, to some extent, has overridden the system's original purpose of favoring the poor.*

Regardless of the truth of that assertion, Social Security has not been a simple retirement savings plan but an instru-

Social Security aims to protect women who stay out of the work force to raise children, offering spousal and

Mr. Carasso and Lee Cohen of the Social Security Administration, a male high-school dropout who retired over the past decade will receive retirement benefits equivalent to his lifetime payroll taxes invested at a 2.7 percent annual rate of return, after accounting for inflation. But for a college graduate, the implicit rate of return on his payroll taxes is 3.2 percent, because he is expected to live seven years longer.

What would Social Security reform do to all of this? Personal accounts, in which people invested their own money for their own retirement, would not redistribute wealth by themselves.

If poor or uneducated workers were allowed to take their stash as a lump sum, though, dying younger would be less of a financial loss. And depending on how Social Security is brought back into long-term financial balance, the distribution of benefits could be reconfigured substantially.

Cutting benefits by raising the retirement age, the choice of Social Security's reformers in 1983, would penalize poorer workers with shorter life spans. But the system could be skewed to transfer more income to the poor. In a report last year, the Government Accountability Office analyzed a plan designed to restore the system's solvency. It included carving out savings accounts, as Mr. Bush suggests, combined with indexing of benefits to inflation instead of to wages and providing low-income retirees a minimum pension of 120 percent of the poverty line. The G.A.O. found that such a system would redistribute more income from high earners to low earners than Social Security does today.

The G.A.O.'s exercise also underscored how changes in the system could undermine Social Security's original goal of protecting the elderly from poverty. Bringing Social Security to long-term solvency without raising contributions would require cutting benefits. Even if personal accounts earned a 4.6 percent annual rate of return over a worker's career—President Bush's central assumption—overall benefits for the bottom fifth of wage earners would be 4 percent lower than their benefits under the current system.

Republicans Weigh Voter Response to Retirement Plan

By Robin Toner; Marjorie Connelly, Janet Elder, and David E. Rosenbaum, contributing reporters
March 10, 2005

Republicans are having a senior moment.

President Bush's Social Security plan has prompted widespread and persistent anxiety and skepticism among retirees and near-retirees, who could cast a third or more of the vote in next year's midterm elections. Despite Mr. Bush's efforts to neutralize those voters, by promising to leave their benefits untouched, Republicans fear—and Democrats hope—that Republicans could be at risk.

In recent days, several top Republican strategists have been warning lawmakers that they must confront and defuse the anxiety among retirees. In a memorandum this week for the National Republican Congressional Committee, the campaign organization for House Republicans, two leading pollsters said their focus groups "made it quite clear that the issue of Social Security and Social Security reform will be a very important vote determinant, particularly for 55-plus voters."

It added, "For older voters, the views of incumbents and candidates on the issue of Social Security and Social Security reform will be as important or, in some cases, more important than issues like the war, health care and education."

David H. Winston, another pollster advising House and Senate Republicans, said in an interview that while Republicans had succeeded in driving home Mr. Bush's promise to leave the over-55 group alone, it was not enough. That age group still fears what could happen when Congress opens up the 70-year-old pension program, Mr. Winston said.

"This is not a partisan element or an ideological element," he said. "It's just, 'Right now, everything is O.K. and all right, and opening Pandora's box could change it.'"

The stakes for Republicans on Capitol Hill are very high: they have carried the 60-and-over vote for House races in five of the last six elections, though often narrowly. Some Democrats have said that older voters are the main reason they have failed to regain control of Congress. Those voters are especially important in off-year elections because they are much more likely to vote than the young.

This makes some of the polling data particularly worrisome for the Republicans. Polls consistently show that older Americans are far more likely than younger ones to think private investment accounts in Social Security, as Mr. Bush has proposed, are a bad idea. In the most recent New York Times/CBS News poll, in late February, 64 percent of those age 65 and older said allowing people to invest part of their Social Security taxes was a bad idea; 29 percent said it was a good idea.

The starkest contrast was with the youngest age group, those 18 to 30. Only 37 percent of them said personal accounts were a bad idea while 55 percent said they were a good idea.

In short, the idea is most unpopular with the group most likely to vote. "Given the reaction of older voters to this Social Security proposal," said Andrew Kohut, director of the Pew Research Center, "if they stick with it, older voters are going to be at risk for the G.O.P."

Political strategists offer various explanations for the resistance of older voters to the president's plan. They say older voters are generally risk averse, are intimately familiar with the current Social Security system and know how important it is in their lives. In polls for the Pew center, older voters also cited their fears that many people were not up to the task of managing these accounts.

Democrats and some independent analysts say that the Bush strategy may be based on fundamental miscalculations: assuming that older Americans will act largely on the basis of their self-interest, and underestimating their support for the program itself. "They think it worked well for them, and they want to keep it that way for their children and grandchildren," said Senator Charles E. Schumer of New York, chairman of the Democratic Senatorial Campaign Committee.

Moreover, Democrats say that not every retiree accepts Mr. Bush's promise that they will be unaffected. In fact, the Republican campaign memo-randum expressed concern that older voters would be very susceptible to the charge that the cost of setting up personal accounts would take a heavy toll on the solvency of Social Security.

In short, the idea [of Social Security reform] is most unpopular with the group most likely to vote.

"Older respondents have a strongly negative reaction to this information about transition costs," it stated, "and it causes them to become significantly more negative about the potential changes and reforms proposed."

Not surprisingly, several Republican leaders have tried to broaden the debate beyond personal retirement accounts. On Wednesday, at the House Ways and Means Committee's first hearing this year on Social Security, the chairman, Representative Bill Thomas of California, emphasized his intention of opening the debate to include "a re-examination of the government's commitment to an aging society."

The ranking Democrat on the committee, Representative Charles B. Rangel of New York, said Democrats would participate in such discussions only if proposals for private investment accounts funded by Social Security taxes were "off the table."

The Republican challenge with the over-55 vote is all the more daunting because of the opposition of AARP, the retirees' lobby, which has been organiz-ing and advertising heavily against the idea of diverting payroll taxes to create personal investment accounts. The Republican committee memorandum, a general look at the Social Security issue based on 14 focus groups in six cities, underscored the problem:

"AARP is the only messenger with any credibility among 55-plus voters (both 55–64 and 65-plus voters) while there is no individual, organization or entity that has significant credibility on the issue of Social Security among 18–54-year-old voters."

Republican leaders say they believe they can make their case with older voters with persistence, and with appeals to consider the interests of their children and grandchildren. Senator Rick Santorum of Pennsylvania, the No. 3 Republican in the Senate leadership, counsels calm.

"I just think there has to be a consistent message," Mr. Santorum said. "When seniors hear change and Social Security in the same sentence, there's not a positive reaction." But ultimately, he said, Republicans will be judged at election time by what they have actually proposed or voted on, neither of which, he says, will affect people 55 and over.

A Democrat on Bush's Social Security Team

By Eduardo Porter
April 30, 2005

The intellectual force behind President Bush's plan to overhaul Social Security, the man the president calls his favorite "Democrat economist," is not an economist. He is Robert C. Pozen, a lawyer and mutual fund executive who serves as chairman of MFS Investment Management in Boston.

A registered Democrat, Mr. Pozen donated money to the presidential campaign of Senator John Kerry last year and voted for him on Nov. 2. He was a classmate of Hillary Rodham Clinton at Yale Law School.

But all that has not stopped President Bush from embracing Mr. Pozen's main idea to bring the nation's public pension regime into financial balance: a plan called "progressive indexing" because it would protect the lowest-wage workers from benefit reductions while progressively cutting benefits of higher-earning workers.

Mr. Pozen, who served on Mr. Bush's commission in 2001 that developed initial plans for carving private accounts out of Social Security, has been thrust into the spotlight by Mr. Bush's embrace of his proposal. But Mr. Pozen says his ideas on public pensions are free of politics.

certain amount of spreading the blame around for that."

To Democrats, however, Mr. Pozen is just providing the president with political cover.

Mr. Pozen "does not speak for the Democratic Party," said Peter Orszag of the Brookings Institution, a liberal research institution. The president drafted Mr. Pozen onto his commission, Mr. Orszag said, only "because they were looking for Democrats that would restrict themselves to be in favor of private accounts."

Mr. Pozen's support for private accounts seems only natural given his long and successful career as a top-level executive in the fund management business.

cial hole estimated by Social Security actuaries—in today's money—at nearly $4 trillion over 75 years.

Mr. Pozen has said that progressive indexing, which would not start until 2012 under his proposal, would close 70 percent of the estimated gap by substantially limiting benefits for higher-income retirees.

Under the current system, the benefits set at retirement are supposed to grow, on average, at the same pace as wages, so that the comparative living standards of retirees, while generally lower than working Americans, do not erode below today's levels.

Mr. Pozen's plan would maintain that schedule only for the bottom 30 percent of the work force—those with average annual earnings up to $25,000.

At the top, those earning more than the taxable limit—expected to be about $113,000 in 2012 when the plan would start, would have future benefits uncoupled from wages and linked instead to inflation, which tends to grow at a pace about 1.1 percentage points slower than wages. In the middle, benefits would be indexed by a mix of prices and wages.

This re-indexing would substantially reduce benefit growth at the top. Today, for example, an American whose earnings are in line with the maximum income taxed by Social Security, currently $90,000, can expect to receive as much as 42 percent of that amount upon retirement. Mr. Pozen's proposal would steadily reduce that to 22 percent by 2061.

Mr. Pozen argued that personal accounts could be layered on top of this plan, eventually providing additional income. But even as the Bush administration has embraced Mr. Pozen's proposal for progressive indexing, it has steered clear of adopting his plan to raise taxes as part of a Social Security overhaul.

Mr. Pozen has been recommending adding private accounts to Social Security since the mid-1990's, which may have been what brought him to the attention of the Bush White House.

Progressive indexing [of Social Security benefits] would close 70 percent of the estimated gap by substantially limiting benefits for higher-income retirees.

"I consider myself a middle-of-the-road guy who tries to be carefully nonpartisan on this issue," he said. "I believe passionately in Social Security reform."

Opponents of the White House plan say that while Mr. Pozen's ideas may sound progressive, they are far from the Democratic mainstream. Mr. Pozen's proposals are "bad policy," said Senator Max Baucus, the ranking Democrat on the Senate Finance Committee, after the committee's hearings on Social Security this week.

The conservative side of the economics profession lauds progressive indexing. "It is a pretty fair way to approach the problem," said Michael Tanner, who heads the Project on Social Security Choice at the libertarian Cato Institute.

Mr. Tanner pointed to the political wisdom of pegging the plan to a Democratic thinker.

"It will be perceived by some as a benefit cut," he said, "and there is a

After serving a stint as a lawyer at the Securities and Exchange Commission, Mr. Pozen joined Fidelity Investments, the financial powerhouse, in 1987. He left Fidelity 14 years later, substantially richer after rising to the position of vice chairman and after being in charge of the firm's big mutual fund group.

"It's fair to say I'm financially independent," Mr. Pozen said.

Since then, he has served on President Bush's commission, was secretary of economic affairs for Gov. Mitt Romney of Massachusetts, a Republican, and taught at Harvard Law School. He took over as chairman of MFS in 2004 after it was battered by financial turmoil and scandal.

At the Senate Finance Committee hearing this week, Mr. Pozen said that while personal accounts were not essential to solving Social Security's financial woes, they were the "dessert" to be offered to American retirees after they had eaten the "spinach" of benefit cuts needed to plug a finan-

"I'm not sure how I got invited to be a member" of the 2001 commission, Mr. Pozen said, "but I had worked on various Social Security projects over the years."

But now he worries that any plan to overhaul Social Security will fail unless it includes both benefit cuts and tax increases.

"As you know," Mr. Pozen said, "both sides have got to win."

Finances of Social Security and Medicare Deteriorate

By Robert Pear
May 2, 2006

WASHINGTON, MAY 1—The financial condition of Medicare and Social Security deteriorated in the last year, the Bush administration reported Monday, and it warned again that the programs were unsustainable in their current form.

Medicare's hospital insurance trust fund, a widely watched gauge of the program's solvency, will run out of money in 2018, two years earlier than projected in last year's report, the trustees said.

And the Social Security trust fund will be exhausted in 2040, one year earlier than projected last year, the trustees said. At that point, in 2040, Social Security tax collections would be adequate to pay only 74 percent of scheduled benefits.

Lawmakers said they would never allow the trust funds to run dry. But the insolvency dates are a vivid way of showing that the programs are unsustainable. To keep them solvent, Congress would need to trim benefits, raise taxes or take some combination of such steps.

"The systems are going broke," President Bush said Monday in a speech to the American Hospital Association.

Almost every element of the programs reflects a political judgment, but Mr. Bush said, "It's time to set aside politics and restructure Social Security and Medicare for generations to come."

Republicans and Democrats seized on the reports to renew the political

battle over Social Security and Medicare, with an eye to Congressional elections this fall.

The Senate Democratic leader, Harry Reid of Nevada, said the reports showed that "despite White House scare tactics, Social Security remains

The insolvency dates are a vivid way of showing that the programs are unsustainable.

sound for decades to come." Senator Max Baucus, Democrat of Montana, said the administration had worsened Medicare's problems by promoting managed-care plans, which he said often "cost more than traditional Medicare."

The administration urged Congress to approve the president's proposals to slow the growth of Medicare by curbing payments to hospitals. Under current law, the trustees said, doctors already face a cut of 4.7 percent or more in Medicare fees in each of the next nine years.

The trustees' reports are authoritative documents prepared by career civil servants, mainly actuaries, and are full of data used as a basis for policy making and political debate.

In the report on Medicare, the Bush administration reduced its estimates of the number of people who would

sign up for the new prescription drug benefit.

The trustees now predict that 31.4 million people will have signed up for the drug benefit by the end of the initial enrollment period in two weeks, and that monthly enrollment for 2006 will average 29.2 million, down from an estimate of 39 million published in last year's report.

Likewise, the administration now predicts enrollment of 34 million for 2007, down from an estimate of 39.8 million in last year's report.

Treasury Secretary John W. Snow said Medicare's financial problems were more severe than those of Social Security because of "steady large increases in underlying health care costs."

The new report estimates that the basic Medicare premium—what a beneficiary pays for coverage of doctors' services and other outpatient care—will be higher than predicted last year. The premium has increased more than 50 percent in the last three years, to $88.50 a month, from $58.70 in 2003, and the Bush administration predicts that it will rise to $98.20 next year.

By contrast, in last year's report, the administration predicted that the basic 2007 premium would be $87.70.

But the average premiums for drug coverage are lower than expected: $32.20 this year and $35.86 in 2007. The comparable figures in last year's report were $37.37 and $41.22.

The administration lowered its estimate of the cost of the drug benefit for the period from 2006 to 2014. The administration now puts the cost at $872 billion, down from $1.1 trillion last year. (The figures do not reflect premiums paid by beneficiaries or compulsory payments by states to help defray the costs.)

In a joint statement, the public trustees of the two programs, John L. Palmer and Thomas R. Saving, said the projected costs of the drug benefit were "significantly lower than those in the 2005 report due to recent slower growth in overall prescription drug spending and lower enrollment in stand-alone prescription drug plans than was expected a year ago."

Still, the administration said, the cost of the drug benefit will grow an average of 11.5 percent a year in the next decade, more than twice as fast as the economy.

II. PERSPECTIVES ON HEALTH CARE

Health care, now consuming over one-fifth of the nation's economy according to the first article, is in crisis. One the one hand, costs seems to escalate in a manner that is quite difficult to constrain. On the other hand, the number of uninsured continues to grow. Massachusetts has recently designed an answer to the problem of the uninsured as described in the second article; however, there is less assurance that cost containment is certain. Local efforts often prove cost effective as the third article illustrates, but to date, there have been no national proposals that contain plans that both expand coverage and control health care costs. As global competition continues to intrude on domestic markets and threaten the nation's economic well-being, the complexities associated with rising health care costs are challenges that are becoming harder to ignore.

As you read the following articles, consider how you would answer these questions.

5. Health Care, Vexing to Clinton, Is Now at Top of Bush's Agenda (01/29/06)

- What is the difference between Bush's and Clinton's perspectives on health care?
- How have the flaws in the U.S. health care system changed since Clinton was in office?

6. Massachusetts Sets Health Plan for Nearly All (04/05/06)

- What is the "individual mandate" legislated in Massachusetts and why is it important?
- Who were most likely to be uninsured with incomes above 300 percent of the poverty line?

7. Hospitals Try Free Basic Care for Uninsured (10/25/06)

- How can it be less costly for hospitals to provide free care for chronic health conditions?
- How does the current system pit different levels of government against one aother?

8. Health Insurance Industry Urges Expansion of Coverage (11/14/06)

- Who will benefit by this expansion of Medicaid and CHIP health insurance coverage?
- What are the cost containment strategies in this insurance industry proposal?

Health Care, Vexing to Clinton, Is Now at Top of Bush's Agenda

By Robert Pear
January 29, 2006

WASHINGTON, JAN. 28—More than 12 years after President Bill Clinton unveiled his plan to remake the nation's health care system, President Bush is moving the issue once again to the top of the national agenda and is expected to push a series of health care proposals in his State of the Union address on Tuesday.

Where Mr. Clinton was driven by a desire to guarantee health insurance for every American, Mr. Bush is focusing primarily on health costs, which he says are swamping employers and threatening economic growth. Where Mr. Clinton favored a larger role for government, Mr. Bush has a fundamentally different philosophy, built on the idea that placing more responsibility in the hands of individuals will create market pressure to hold down costs.

The long-running debate has taken on new urgency as more and more companies find themselves struggling to pay for employee health benefits. Health care costs have been a big factor in the troubles of the domestic auto industry, among others.

But some policy experts, Republicans and Democrats alike, say the Bush proposals, which are built around tax breaks, may further drive up health spending and costs by fueling the demand for health care. Such unintended effects show how difficult it is to apply economic theory to the complexities of the current health care system.

By making health care a prominent theme of his prime-time address to the nation, Mr. Bush hopes to regain the initiative on domestic policy. Success with his health care proposals, after the failure of his effort to overhaul Social Security, would allow the president to build political momentum heading into the midterm elections this fall.

The White House has indicated that Mr. Bush will propose tax deductions for out-of-pocket medical expenses, rules to encourage the use of health savings accounts and incentives for small businesses across the country to band together and buy health insurance, exempt from state regulation.

Regina E. Herzlinger, a professor at Harvard Business School, said: "Insuring the uninsured is a fine objective, but how will this control the health costs that are hobbling our global competitiveness? Health savings accounts will increase coverage, and that's great. But they are being touted as a way to control costs, and I very much doubt that claim."

Democrats see the Bush proposals as a pastiche of old and new ideas that falls far short of what is required to tame the explosive growth in health costs.

Many economists say that the tax code, by subsidizing the purchase of health insurance, has fostered excessive use of health care services, driving up costs. Rather than proposing any limit on this subsidy, Mr. Bush wants to make it more widely available, to people who buy health care and insurance on their own.

Under current law, employers who pay health insurance premiums for employees can deduct the payments as a business expense on their tax returns, and the payments are not counted as taxable income for the employees. But such subsidies are unavailable to people who buy insurance themselves. President Bush sees that difference as unfair.

Allan B. Hubbard, assistant to the president for economic policy, said, "Health care purchased by an employer is done on a pretax basis, before your payroll taxes, before your income taxes.

If you work for an employer who cannot afford to provide health insurance and so you go out and buy it, you have to use after-tax dollars."

In an interview, Mr. Hubbard continued: "Another unfairness is that if you buy health care with your insurance, you use pretax dollars. If you pay for it out of pocket, you have to use after-tax dollars. That encourages you to insure health care events that are routine. Insurance was never created to deal with the routine."

People use health savings accounts to pay routine medical expenses and buy high-deductible insurance policies to cover larger expenses. Mr. Bush says this arrangement encourages people to take more responsibility for all aspects of their care, including its cost.

"It's the opposite of federal control," Mr. Bush told a group of small-business owners this month. "It is patient control."

The White House had been hoping to highlight the new Medicare drug benefit as a model, showing how private health plans could deliver better benefits at lower cost than the government. But if Mr. Bush mentions it in his State of the Union address, he will invite catcalls from Democrats.

Senator Richard J. Durbin of Illinois, the assistant Democratic leader, said the drug benefit had become "a fiasco, a disaster," because it was written by Republicans who placed too much trust in private markets.

Representative Nancy Pelosi of California, the House Democratic leader, said, "Health savings accounts are brought to you by the same people who brought you the confusing, special-interest-driven Medicare prescription drug bill."

Health policy experts raise many questions about Mr. Bush's proposals: Would the new tax breaks go to people who already had insurance or would buy it anyway? Would they undermine the system of employer-provided health insurance? Would healthy individuals be more likely to take the new options, leaving employers to pay for sick people with higher health costs?

Stuart M. Butler, a vice president of the conservative Heritage Foundation, said Mr. Bush was focusing more on costs than on coverage for the uninsured. The tax proposals, he said, are "a bit of a gamble," forced on the president by the bizarre politics of health care.

Jonathan Gruber, a professor of economics at the Massachusetts Institute of Technology who worked at the Treasury under President Clinton, said, "The new tax breaks would be expensive and regressive, offering the largest benefits to the highest-income taxpayers."

In diagnosing flaws in the health care system, Mr. Bush could lift whole sentences from Mr. Clinton's address to a joint session of Congress on Sept. 22, 1993.

Opening his campaign for "health security," Mr. Clinton said, "Our medical bills are growing at over twice the rate of inflation." He warned that "rising costs are a special nightmare for our small businesses," and that "health care costs will devour more and more and more of our budget."

The Clinton plan died in Congress, after months of criticism from small businesses, health insurance companies and Republicans, who called it a costly, complex "big government" scheme.

Since then, national health spending has doubled, to $1.9 trillion. Health care now accounts for one-sixth of the nation's economy. Medicare and Medicaid, which accounted for 15.5 percent of federal spending in 1993, now consume almost 21 percent.

In Mr. Bush's first term, the number of people without health insurance increased more than a million a year, to 45.8 million in 2004, the last year for which official figures were available.

Democrats and consumer groups led the campaign for health care legislation in 1993. Now business executives and small-business owners express a similar sense of urgency.

In his recent meeting with small-business owners, Mr. Bush said, "Government policy has got to aim at the increasing cost of health care." The number of uninsured is rising because health costs are going up, he said, "so the government needs to address the cost."

While they are not required to provide health benefits, many large employers are committed to doing so, despite the rapidly rising costs. Employers see health benefits as a way to attract workers and to keep them productive, said E. Neil Trautwein, assistant vice president of the National Association of Manufacturers.

Over the years, many employers have become expert in buying health coverage for employees, and they do not want to drop this responsibility or dismantle the current system.

But employers have been clamoring for policy makers to address the needs of the uninsured. Employers say they indirectly pay for the uninsured, because the cost of their care is factored into the prices charged by hospitals and other health care providers.

"The health care cost crisis has a lot to do with the growing number of uninsured," said Katie W. Mahoney, manager of health policy at the United States Chamber of Commerce.

Health costs are swamping employers and threatening economic growth.

Massachusetts Sets Health Plan for Nearly All

By Pam Belluck; Katie Zezima, contributing reporter
April 5, 2006

BOSTON, APRIL 4—Massachusetts is poised to become the first state to provide nearly universal health care coverage with a bill passed overwhelmingly by the legislature Tuesday that Gov. Mitt Romney says he will sign.

The bill does what health experts say no other state has been able to do: provide a mechanism for all of its citizens to obtain health insurance. It accomplishes that in a way that experts say combines methods and proposals from across the political spectrum, apportioning the cost among businesses, individuals and the government.

"This is probably about as close as you can get to universal," said Paul B. Ginsburg, president of the nonpartisan Center for Studying Health System Change in Washington. "It's definitely going to be inspiring to other states about how there was this compromise. They found a way to get to a major expansion of coverage that people could agree on. For a conservative Republican, this is individual responsibility. For a Democrat, this is government helping those that need help."

The bill, the product of months of wrangling between legislators and the governor, requires all Massachusetts residents to obtain health coverage by July 1, 2007.

Individuals who can afford private insurance will be penalized on their state income taxes if they do not purchase it. Government subsidies to private insurance plans will allow more of the working poor to buy insurance and will expand the number of children who are eligible for free coverage. Businesses with more than 10 workers that do not provide insurance will be assessed up to $295 per employee per year.

All told, the plan is expected to cover 515,000 uninsured people within three years, about 95 percent of the state's uninsured population, legislators said, leaving less than 1 percent of the population unprotected.

"It is not a typical Massachusetts-Taxachusetts, oh-just-crazy-liberal plan," said Stuart H. Altman, a professor of health policy at Brandeis University. "It isn't that at all. It is a pretty moderate approach, and that's what's impressive about it. It tried to borrow and blend a lot of different pieces."

Many states, including Massachusetts, have been wrestling for years with how to cover the uninsured, and several states have come close, according to the National Conference of State Legislatures. Hawaii passed a universal access law in 1974 requiring employers to offer health care coverage for employees working 20 hours or more a week, but nearly 10 percent of people remain uncovered. Efforts to cover all citizens in Minnesota and Vermont in 1992 and in Massachusetts in 1988 fell flat in the mid-1990s when the language in the bills concerning universal coverage was repealed.

In 2003, Maine enacted a law that significantly broadened insurance coverage and combined employer payments with expanded government programs. That year, California enacted a

law that required employer contributions, but it was repealed in a referendum in 2004. Massachusetts would be the first state to require its citizens to have health insurance.

The Massachusetts bill creates a sliding scale of affordability ranging from people who can afford insurance outright to those who cannot afford it at all. About 215,000 people will be covered by allowing individuals and businesses with 50 or fewer employees to buy insurance with pretax dollars, and by giving insurance companies incentives to offer stripped-down plans at lower cost. Lower-cost basic plans will be available to people ages 19 to 26.

Subsidies for other private plans will be available for people with incomes at or below 300 percent of the poverty level. Children in those families will be eligible for free coverage through Medicaid, an expansion of the current system.

a successful exercise," said State Senator Robert E. Travaglini, the majority leader.

Mr. Romney, who is considering running for president in 2008, said in an interview Tuesday that the bill, passed by a legislature that is 85 percent Democratic, was "95 percent of what I proposed."

He said, "This is really a landmark for our state because this proves at this stage that we can get health insurance for all our citizens without raising taxes and without a government takeover. The old single-payer canard is gone."

Mr. Romney pushed the idea of the "individual mandate," requiring people who can afford insurance to buy it. The bill makes it possible for employers to enable many of those people to use pretax dollars, saving them 25 percent or more. Individuals who fail to get health insurance by July 2007 will first

All told, the plan is expected to cover 515,000 uninsured people within three years, about 95 percent of the state's uninsured population.

The Massachusetts bill was hammered out with proposals and input from state Democratic legislators; Mr. Romney, a Republican; Senator Edward M. Kennedy, a Democrat; insurers; academics; businesses; hospitals; and advocates for the poor, including religious leaders.

They were motivated in part by a threat by the federal government to eliminate $385 million in federal Medicaid money unless the state reduced the number of uninsured people. The state was supposed to have the bill completed by January, but state officials said they were confident that the federal government would approve of Tuesday's bill.

"Whenever you can have the medical community, the business community and the advocates all applauding our efforts, I think that's indicative of

lose their personal exemption on their state taxes. In subsequent years, they would have to pay a penalty that could be as high as half of what an affordable health care premium would cost.

Eric Fehrnstrom, the governor's communications director, said that for those people with incomes above 300 percent of poverty, "our assumption was that these would be mostly single mothers who just did not have the wherewithal to get insurance. It turned out it was mostly young males. In some cases they are making very attractive salaries. These are people who just don't imagine themselves needing care, but of course when they break a leg when they're out bungee jumping they go to the hospital and we end up paying for their care anyway."

One element that Mr. Romney and some legislators did not want was the fee for employers who do not provide health insurance.

For several months the bill seemed stalled because the House and Senate leaders could not agree on the issue of charging businesses. One proposal of an $800-per-employee charge was reduced to a maximum of $295 that would go toward paying costs for the uninsured and would be reduced as more people became insured, Mr. Travaglini said.

Because the bill is part of a budget bill, Mr. Romney has line-item veto power. He said Tuesday that he would likely change the business fee provision in some way or veto it before signing the bill.

Still, he did not seem that worried about it, saying he had been most concerned that the fee not be a payroll tax, as had been originally proposed. Mr. Travaglini said that if Mr. Romney vetoed the business fee, the legislature would override it.

Bob Baker, president of the Smaller Business Association of New England, said his members seemed to accept the idea of the fee.

"The notion of the level playing field, I think from an element of fairness and equity, people are O.K. with it, unless it impinges on their ability to pay for it," Mr. Baker said. "There hasn't been a hue and cry among our members."

Mr. Romney said that with more people insured, everyone would "get better health care" and that premiums for people who already had insurance might drop because "providers won't be pushing the cost of the uninsured onto the people who have insurance."

James Roosevelt Jr., president and chief executive of Tufts Health Plan, agreed.

"I think that will help both improve the quality of health care and lower the cost," Mr. Roosevelt said, but he added, "We would have liked more flexibility in the design of health plans to permit lower premiums that are affordable for all people."

The program, which was approved 154 to 2 in the House and 37 to 0 in the Senate, will cost $1.2 billion over three years, but only $125 million of

that will be new state money. The rest will come from federal money and existing state money. After three years, lawmakers say, no new state money will be required. A new agency will administer the system.

Advocates for the uninsured held a victory rally at the Statehouse.

"We're thrilled that this truly represents a commitment to the poor and the working poor," said Rabbi Jonah Pesner, a leader of the Greater Boston Interfaith Organization.

Joseph Landais, 64, could use insurance for himself, his wife and three children. Mr. Landais, a retired hospital custodian, said his wife, a nurse's aide, makes too much for the family to be eligible for Medicaid but not enough to afford insurance. He had a hernia operation four months ago that he did not have to pay for under the free-care pool, but he had not been able to see a doctor since then, even though he is still not feeling well.

"After years that you've been working that hard," Mr. Landais said, "I think you deserve something back."

Hospitals Try Free Basic Care for Uninsured

By Erik Eckholm
October 25, 2006
(Correction Appended)

AUSTIN, TEX. — Unable to afford health insurance, Dee Dee Dodd had for years been mixing occasional doctor visits with clumsy efforts to self-manage her insulin-dependent diabetes, getting sicker all the while.

In one 18-month period, Ms. Dodd, 38, was rushed almost monthly to the emergency room, spent weeks in the intensive care unit and accumulated more than $191,000 in unpaid bills.

That is when nurses at the Seton Family of Hospitals tagged her as a "frequent flier," a repeat visitor whose ailments—and expenses—might be curbed with more regular care. The

hospital began offering her free primary care through its charity program.

With the number of uninsured people in the United States reaching a record 46.6 million last year, up by 7 million from 2000, Seton is one of a small number of hospital systems around the country to have done the math and acted on it. Officials decided that for many patients with chronic diseases, it would be cheaper to provide free preventive care than to absorb the high cost of repeated emergencies.

With patients like Ms. Dodd, "they can have better care and we can reduce the costs for the hospital," said

Dr. Melissa Smith, medical director of three community health centers run by Seton, a Roman Catholic hospital network that uses its profits and donations to provide nearly free care to 5,000 of the working poor. Over the last 18 months, Ms. Dodd's health has improved, and her medical bills have been cut nearly in half.

Reaching out to uninsured patients, especially those with chronic conditions like diabetes, hypertension, congestive heart failure or asthma, is a recent tactic of "a handful of visionary hospital systems around the country," said Karen Davis, president of the

Commonwealth Fund, a foundation in New York that concentrates on health care. These institutions are searching for ways to fend off disease and large debts by bringing uninsured visitors into continuing basic care.

The public hospital systems in New York and Denver, for example, have both worked to steer uninsured patients to community clinics, charging modest fees, if any. New York's public system, the Health and Hospitals Corporation, has assigned some 240,000 uninsured patients to personal primary care doctors. A computerized system tracks those with chronic conditions, and when necessary, social workers contact patients to make sure they get checkups and follow medical advice.

"For most preventive efforts there is an upfront expense," said Alan D. Aviles, president of the corporation. "But over the long term it saves money."

Denver's public system, Denver Health, has 41,000 uninsured patients enrolled in its clinics. Officials there calculate that for every dollar they spend on prenatal care for uninsured women, they save more than $7 in newborn and child care.

The "safety net" plan of the Seton system in Central Texas accepts people making 150 percent to 250 percent of the federal poverty limit and has resources to support 5,000 patients. (People below the poverty line, which is $13,200 a year for a family of two in the contiguous states, can obtain care through the public clinic system.)

Officials scrutinize the records of plan members to see who is still overusing the emergency room or being repeatedly hospitalized—these high-cost patients total some 40 each month—then assign them caseworkers to help improve care and bring down costs.

A special effort to educate 631 asthma patients saved the plan $475,000 in one year, Seton officials said.

In a more unusual step, Seton officials also look for frequent emergency room users who do not qualify for the hospital's charity plan because they live in a different county, like Ms. Dodd, or have incomes just above the threshold. In a dozen cases so far, all involving diabetics, a committee has judged that it makes financial sense to bring these people into the charity plan anyway and provide intensive support.

Other answers to the insurance crisis are being tried around the country, including the creation of subsidized, bare-bones policies for small businesses. Vermont, Maine and especially Massachusetts are using combinations of state and federal money and employer mandates to extend insurance.

Still, only a fraction of the uninsured, in Central Texas and in most other states, are benefiting.

"All these local efforts are commendable, but they are like sticking fingers in the dikes," Ms. Davis of the Commonwealth Fund said, noting that the larger trend was hospitals' seeking to avoid the uninsured.

Nowhere is the problem more acute than in Texas, where nearly a quarter of the population is uninsured, the nation's highest rate. Small businesses here are unlikely to offer benefits, and the state government's unusually stringent restrictions on Medicaid for adults leave many of the working poor at risk.

Even without counting the large immigrant population, Texas has the country's highest share of uninsured, at 21 percent, according to the Center for Public Policy Priorities in Austin.

"All the hospitals here provide some uncompensated care, and they are eating it and passing the costs along to the payers," said Patricia A. Young Brown, president of the Travis County Healthcare District, which was set up last year to oversee care of the indigent through public clinics, drawing on property taxes to pay.

"So insurance rates go up, and then more businesses drop insurance," Ms. Young Brown continued, describing a trend unfolding nationwide. "It's hard to see where it will end. We hear a cry for national and state leadership."

"But it's not a solution to have such a ragtag, makeshift system."

The private People's Community Clinic, supported in part by the St. David's Hospital system, gives primary care to 11,000 people in Austin who are uninsured or on Medicaid and related programs.

"I think we are a good Band-Aid for those able to come to our clinic," Regina Rogoff, director of the clinic, said. "But it's not a solution to have such a ragtag, makeshift system."

Austin hospitals and charity clinics have also joined in a pioneering data-sharing system to track visits by uninsured patients and fight unnecessary use of the emergency room. But rural counties in Texas offer little aid, and rural residents with serious maladies end up traveling to urban emergency rooms.

The current patchwork also pits different levels of government against each other.

Natavidad Martinez, 51, who used to work as a bookbinder for $7 an hour and never had insurance, has found herself in a bureaucratic nightmare.

In March 2005, Ms. Martinez, a Seton patient, was found to have liver cancer. She was put on Medicaid, applied for federal disability and was put in line for a liver transplant, without which, doctors said, she had six months to two years to live. Through the summer of 2005, she made the hour-and-a-half drive from her home to San Antonio for preparatory tests.

That August, she was awarded disability payments of $561 a month. But because her income surpassed the $535 limit for Medicaid in her circumstances, she said, she was told by the state that her coverage had ended, and the hospital said it could not proceed with a transplant.

"I asked Social Security if they couldn't just reduce my payments by $30 a month," she said, "but they said it doesn't work that way."

In another twist, by federal rules, she will qualify for Medicare two years after the initial finding of disability. She awaits the start of Medicare coverage next March, when she can rejoin the transplant line.

In Texas, as throughout the country, the coverage of poor children through Medicaid and related programs expanded greatly over the last decade. But a majority of states do not provide Medicaid to parents making even poverty-line incomes, and Texas is one of the least generous: here, a working parent of two does not qualify for coverage if he or she makes more than $3,696 in a year, leaving people like Ms. Dodd to fend for themselves.

Ms. Dodd, who worked as a dental assistant, is married to a truck driver, has four children and lives on a country road in Hays County, south of Austin. Ten years ago, after her weight fell to 82 pounds, she learned that she was a "brittle diabetic," subject to rapid and dangerous changes in blood sugar. She saw a doctor only sporadically because visits cost $120—money she did not have.

"I had to stop working, so then I couldn't afford to go to the doctor, and then I had to go to the emergency room," Ms. Dodd said.

She was having repeated episodes of ketoacidosis, a chemical imbalance that sometimes put her into life-threatening comas. Years of poor care had weakened her and led to side effects like esophogeal ulcers that could probably have been prevented, her doctors said.

Ms. Dodd still has problems, but the use of a $3,200 insulin pump paid for by Seton, which automatically adjusts her insulin levels, along with access to an endocrinologist and home counseling have reduced their severity. Her care in the last 18 months has cost Seton $104,697, far below the $191,277 for the previous period. More important, the later figures include less hospital time and more medicines and expert advice.

"The money we save," Dr. Smith, of Seton, said, "money that is not hemorrhaging through the I.C.U., is money we can do so much more with to help her upfront."

■ **Correction:** Oct. 26, 2006. A front-page article yesterday about hospitals that offer free basic care to the uninsured referred incorrectly to the 47 million uninsured people in the United States. The figure includes noncitizens; they are not all Americans.

Health Insurance Industry Urges Expansion of Coverage

By Robert Pear
November 14, 2006

The health insurance industry proposed an expansion of Medicaid and new tax breaks on Monday with the goal of guaranteeing coverage for all children in three years and for virtually all adults within 10 years.

New members of Congress, especially those elected on a pledge to help the uninsured, are likely to embrace many of the proposals, which provide a benchmark for debate on the issue. The debate is likely to rage in the next Congress and in the 2008 presidential campaign.

The latest government figures show that 46.6 million Americans lacked health insurance in 2005, an increase of 17 percent, or 6.8 million, from 2000.

"We believe that every American should have access to affordable health care coverage," said J. Grover Thomas Jr., chairman of America's Health Insurance Plans, the main lobby for the industry, which offered the proposals.

The industry proposed these steps, estimated to cost $300 billion over 10 years:

- The federal government and the states should expand Medicaid to cover all adults with annual incomes under the poverty level, including single adults who cannot now qualify. The poverty level is $16,600 for a family of three and $9,800 for an individual.
- The Children's Health Insurance Program, financed jointly by the federal government and the states, should, at a minimum, cover all children in families with incomes less than twice the poverty level.
- Congress should create tax incentives for people to establish "universal health accounts." People could take tax deductions for amounts contributed to such accounts. They could use the accounts to pay premiums for any type of health insurance. The federal government would help pay premiums for people with incomes below certain levels.
- Congress should establish a tax credit for individuals and families who buy health insurance for their children. The credit would be $200 a child, up to a maximum of $500 for a family. It would be available to families with incomes up to three times the poverty level—up to $60,000 for a family of four.

The industry did not say how its proposals would be paid for; did not recommend any budget cuts or tax increases; and did not say what, if anything, it would do to slow the growth of health costs.

When hospitals care for the uninsured, they often pass on some of the costs to people who have health insurance. Jay M. Gellert, president of Health Net, a managed-care company based in Woodland Hills, Calif., said this "cost shift" threatened to make coverage unaffordable for employers, who provide health benefits to 175 million people.

Ronald F. Pollack, the executive director of Families USA, a liberal-leaning consumer group, said: "Given the insurance industry's history as a major opponent of health care reform in 1993–94, this set of proposals is very welcome. The proposals for public programs, in particular, are laudable."

Grace-Marie Turner, president of the Galen Institute, a research center that advocates free-market health policies, said: "Conservatives will be able to support this. It has something for everyone."

Under current law, employers can generally take tax deductions for the cost of providing health benefits to employees. The industry plan calls for a similar deduction for people who buy coverage on their own, in the individual health insurance market.

In a sense, insurers, like other industries, are recommending tax subsidies for the products they sell. More generally, they are proposing a public-private partnership to cope with a problem — the soaring cost of health care and health insurance — that affects families, employers and the nation's ability to compete in a global economy.

"We are the last industrialized country in the world not to have universal coverage," said George C. Halvorson, chairman of the Kaiser Permanente health plan.

Many economists say the tax code is biased against individual insurance. The industry said it was proposing "full tax deductibilty for health insurance premiums" to correct the bias.

C. Eugene Steuerle, a senior fellow at the Urban Institute, said he worried that such a change could create incentives for some employees to buy insurance on their own, rather than through the workplace. "Unless carefully designed," he said, "that change could

"We are the last industrialized country in the world not to have universal coverage."

reduce the incentives for employers to provide coverage, and we could get a net increase in the number of people without insurance."

Mr. Thomas, who is chairman of Trustmark Mutual Holding Company, based in Lake Forest, Ill., said this concern was unfounded. Workers would generally lose the employer's subsidy for their health care if they bought insurance outside the workplace, he said.

Many economists say the tax code, by subsidizing the purchase of health insurance, has fostered excessive use of health care services, driving up costs. "New subsidies could aggravate that problem," Mr. Steuerle said.

III. PERSPECTIVES ON WELFARE AND WORK

Who are the poor? As the first article explains, this question is a bit harder to answer than it may appear. What is certain is that the metric used to determine the poverty line is clearly out of date. It is also difficult to associate poverty with welfare as the second article describes. Declining welfare rolls do not result only from increases in family incomes, and the plight of the working poor is too often neglected. The third article focuses on the inability of current welfare reforms to solve the poverty of the neediest, and despite the federal requirements described in the fourth article that requires states to achieve higher levels of success in moving welfare recipients to work, there seems to be little focus on the growing population that is both working and poor. Welfare reform has become a version of labor policy, but there remain problems in training and placement for many as the last article illustrates. Work requirements that are not coupled to a livable minimum wage constitute a form of corporate welfare. Low wages tend to enrich the companies who do not have to pay their employees fairly. Is this fair and just?

As you read the following articles, consider how you would answer these questions.

9. Economic View: A Poverty Line That's Out of Date and Out of Favor (03/12/06)

- Who has responsibility for setting the poverty line, and how does this influence its accuracy?
- What changes in the poverty line calculations have been suggested?

10. Welfare Rolls Falling Again, Amid Worries about Poverty (04/06/06)

- Why are some concerned that welfare rolls are falling in New York City?
- What three factors explain the decline in welfare rolls?

11. For the Neediest of the Needy, Welfare Reforms Still Fall Short, Study Says (05/17/06)

- What are the barriers to work discovered in Wisconsin?
- What percent of welfare applicants were investigated for child abuse or neglect?

12. New Rules Will Require States to Move Welfare Recipients to Work (06/28/06)

- What do the new rules require for the first time?
- Why are the new rules being criticized for creating a "perverse incentive"?

13. A Welfare Law Milestone Finds Many Left Behind (08/22/06)

- How effective has welfare reform been for Mysheda and her children?
- Who are the "disconnected?"

Economic View: A Poverty Line That's Out of Date and Out of Favor

By Anna Bernasek
March 12, 2006

Before every flight, pilots reset the altimeter of their aircraft to match the elevation of the local airport. If they didn't, the altimeter reading would gradually diverge from the true measure, endangering the safety of all aboard.

It's no different for economic statistics. When they are not updated, the subjects they once measured can become obscured.

A good example is the poverty line, the nation's official measure of need. Economists have long argued that the poverty line should be revised to provide an accurate picture of who is actually poor. Yet it has remained essentially untouched since 1963, when Mollie Orshansky, an economist at the Social Security Administration, first came up with it.

Today, there is a consensus among economists that it is no longer on the mark. "Everyone agrees we need a better measure," said Douglas J. Besharov, a resident scholar at the American Enterprise Institute and a professor of public policy at the University of Maryland.

To him and many others, the public lacks an accurate test of who is poor, making it far harder to justify actions,

that it would be used today as a trigger for billions of dollars in government spending.

Her method was to use the cost of a nutritionally adequate diet as the basis for a cost-of-living estimate and to adjust for families of various sizes and compositions.

Using data from the late 1950's, she estimated that families spent about one-third of their income on food, on average. To come up with a poverty threshold, she multiplied the cost of the nutritionally adequate diet by three.

Each year, the official threshold is adjusted for inflation. The poverty line for a single person under 65 is now $10,160 in annual income, before taxes; for a family of four, it's $19,806. According to the United States Census Bureau, the total number of Americans living in poverty in 2004 was 37 million.

The thresholds have risen over the years to reflect broad price changes, but the assumptions made by Ms. Orshansky remain intact.

Still, much has changed since the 1950's. Today, families spend something close to 12 percent of income on food, for example, not one-third. And while some of the remaining 88 percent

is seen as a national achievement, and an increase in poverty as a sign of problems.

Day to day, the poverty measure directly affects the lives of millions of Americans. At least $60 billion in federal aid annually is linked to the poverty measure, and $260 billion or so in Medicaid spending takes it into account. At the state and local level, thousands of government programs use the poverty line to determine eligibility.

So why hasn't such an important statistic been updated to reflect modern conditions? The answer is politics. Thanks to a quirk of history, the poverty indicator, unlike many other economic statistics, is not under the jurisdiction of an authoritative statistical agency like the Bureau of Economic Analysis or the Bureau of Labor Statistics.

Instead, it resides in perhaps the most political place of all: the office of the president. And during the last four decades, no president of either party has wanted to draw attention to a statistic that the nation has come to take for granted, especially if updating it might cause the number of people regarded as living in poverty to increase.

Ideology, meanwhile, has muddied the debate about how to improve the poverty count. Some experts have tended to advocate adjustments that raise the poverty line, while others prefer ways that decrease it.

This kind of goal-seeking has led many experts to throw up their hands in defeat. "I've come to the conclusion that the official measure is set in stone," Professor Besharov said. He suggests keeping the official measure in place while introducing additional ways of tracking poverty.

But why not insist on an official yardstick that works—especially when

Today, families spend something close to 12 percent of income on food, for example, not one-third.

whether by government or by individuals, intended to alleviate poverty.

No one blames Ms. Orshansky. She devised a simple and elegant measure of poverty based on the data available at the time. And she never expected

may go to nonessentials, items such as housing, transportation and health care are significant, and expensive, factors.

Much is at stake. The poverty line is widely viewed as an indicator of social progress. A decline in poverty

obvious improvements can readily be made?

Rebecca M. Blank, dean of the Gerald R. Ford School of Public Policy at the University of Michigan and a professor of economics, says she thinks that such a yardstick is possible.

She was a member of the National Academy of Sciences panel on poverty and family assistance, which in 1995 conducted the latest official comprehensive study on the topic.

She has found that while no single statistic perfectly captures all of those living in poverty, some straightforward steps could be taken to improve the official indicator. "We really can have a measure today that conceptually makes sense," she said.

Ms. Blank says three changes would provide much help. First, refine what's meant by income. The current gauge uses a family's pretax income. Instead, most economists agree that taxes should be subtracted and near-cash income, such as food stamps, should be added in.

A little less clear is how to deal with the effects of mandatory work expenses, like those for transportation and child care, on income. But Ms. Blank argues that the profession has good tools to come up with reasonable estimates for both.

Her second step would be to update existing thresholds to take into account not only food but also housing, clothing and out-of-pocket medical costs.

And finally, she said, the scales that are used to adjust for differences in family size and composition should be more precise. These steps are largely consistent with recommendations of the National Academy of Sciences report.

The Census Bureau has been tracking alternative measures derived from the academy's recommendations. The bureau found that if such measures had been used in 2003, the latest period for which alternative statistics are available, the poverty rate would have risen about two percentage points above the official rate of 12.5 percent. That's not a big adjustment in percentage terms, but it would add more than five million people to the current poverty count.

Fortunately for a vast majority of Americans, the exact placement of the poverty line is not a matter of everyday concern. That's why it hasn't been a big priority for presidents. But for some Americans living under economic stress who are not now considered poor, updating the gauge could make a tangible difference.

Perhaps the first step in resetting the safety net's altimeter is to take the poverty measure out of the White House and put it in the hands of professional statisticians.

Welfare Rolls Falling Again, Amid Worries about Poverty

By Sewell Chan
April 6, 2006

The number of New York City residents receiving public assistance fell to 402,281 last month, the lowest number since December 1964, at the start of President Lyndon B. Johnson's war on poverty, and a decline of nearly two-thirds from its peak of nearly 1.2 million in March 1995, officials announced yesterday.

After falling sharply during the mayoralty of Rudolph W. Giuliani, when more than 600,000 people left the rolls, the city's caseload began to creep upward in September 2002, during Mayor Michael R. Bloomberg's first year in office and on the tail of a national recession. The modest increases continued until October 2004, when the caseload figure again started to decline.

The recent drop in the number of welfare recipients in the city comes months before the 10th anniversary of the federal welfare overhaul that imposed a five-year limit on assistance, established work requirements and gave states discretion in setting welfare policy. Nationally, the caseload has fallen by more than half since the federal law was signed in August 1996.

The decline in the caseload is occurring amid concerns about income inequality, which has risen more sharply in the city than in the nation as a whole, and new signs that poor families are having a harder time meeting housing and food costs. Last month, Mr. Bloomberg appointed a 32-member Commission for Economic Opportunity to come up with public and private solutions to poverty in the city.

"When I came into office, we were going into an economic slump, and most people thought that the welfare rolls would go up," Mr. Bloomberg said yesterday. "The truth of the matter is, they have gone down."

But welfare recipients who do find work are often in low-paying jobs with limited opportunities for advancement. Of those who have left welfare for work in the city, 88 percent have kept their jobs after three months and 75 percent after six months.

Isabel V. Sawhill, a senior fellow at the Brookings Institution, a research organization in Washington, said the broad decline in welfare caseloads in the last decade could be attributed to three factors: an unusually strong economy in the late 1990's; the federal overhaul that encouraged recipients to find work and financially penalized those who did not; and policies that expanded access to food stamps, child-care subsidies and the earned-income tax credit.

The city's caseload decline since 2004 is surprising because the national caseload decline has slowed significantly, said Gordon L. Berlin, president of MDRC, formerly the Manpower Demonstration Research Corporation, a group in New York and Oakland, Calif., that evaluates social programs.

"The economy has begun to pick up," Mr. Berlin said, "and that's certainly part of the story in New York."

Welfare has been a less prominent issue under Mr. Bloomberg than under Mr. Giuliani, even though the city has maintained the welfare policies started in the mid-1990's. Mr. Giuliani imposed tough eligibility-verification reviews that removed many recipients from the rolls. He also converted welfare offices into job-search centers and required recipients to join the city's Work Experience Program, which placed them in jobs like raking leaves or answering phones. Welfare caseworkers are now called "job opportunity specialists."

"Giuliani gloried in opposing the activist groups and challenging the welfare culture," said Lawrence M. Mead III, a professor of politics at New York University. "The Bloomberg administration continued the Giuliani policies, although without the contentious rhetoric. The change under Bloomberg has been more atmospheric than substantive."

Welfare caseworkers are now called "job opportunity specialists."

In February 2005, the city's Human Resources Administration began WeCare, which provides medical and psychological assessment and care for recipients who have been unable to find work.

Verna Eggleston, the commissioner of the agency, said it had "abandoned the 'one-size-fits-all' social service program model" in favor of an "individualized model."

WeCare has enrolled about 15,000 adults and is expected to serve 40,000 eventually, said Patricia M. Smith, who has worked for the welfare agency since 1974 and is now its first deputy commissioner.

"We've recognized the shift in the demographics and characteristics of the caseload since the early days of welfare reform," she said, adding that many current recipients have "multiple barriers to employment."

The mayor acknowledged the same problem. "I don't think it's realistic to think that everybody can go to work," he said, "but we are going in the right direction."

Gail B. Nayowith, executive director of the Citizens' Committee for Children of New York and a member of the mayor's commission, said the focus needed to shift to economic security from welfare reform. "Parents are working full time and still poor," she said. "There has to be a greater effort on making work pay."

City Councilman Bill de Blasio, a Brooklyn Democrat who is chairman of the Council's General Welfare Committee, said the decline in the caseload was "very good news" but added that "people who've exhausted their benefits have not necessarily found steady income." In 2004, 20.3 percent of residents and 17.4 percent of families in New York City lived below the poverty line.

Mr. de Blasio and advocates for the poor have estimated that there are hundreds of thousands of residents who are eligible for food stamps or for government earned-income tax credits but have not enrolled. Ms. Smith said the welfare agency was allowing people for the first time to apply for benefits through nonprofit groups and that enrollment in another program, Medicaid, had significantly risen.

For the Neediest of the Needy, Welfare Reforms Still Fall Short, Study Says

By Erik Eckholm
May 17, 2006
(Correction Appended)

Several years into Wisconsin's stringent welfare-to-work program, which helped reduce welfare rolls in the state by 80 percent, the remaining welfare recipients fared poorly, seldom finding steady jobs or stable lives, according to a new study that spotlights the severe personal problems afflicting the poorest families.

Wisconsin was a pioneer in welfare reforms adopted by Congress in 1996, imposing work requirements and limits on cash assistance while providing child care, tax credits and other supports for working mothers.

The overhaul, in Wisconsin and other states, helped place more single parents in jobs. But the new study points to another national legacy: the often critical needs of those still seeking aid, who may encounter profound barriers to work that include disabilities or problems with mental health or substance abuse.

"The mix of people the welfare office serves has changed radically," Mark E. Courtney, chief author of the study, said in an interview. "The population that remains is, on average, a much needier population, and they were not helped."

Perhaps the most alarming finding was that because of neglect or abuse, a child was removed from the home of one in every six parents during the five years after they applied for welfare.

Dr. Courtney, director of the Chapin Hall Center for Children at the Univer-

wisdom of "program improvements that we have made in the last three years," including closer screening and broader aid for welfare recipients.

Dr. Courtney agreed that Wisconsin had improved its social services for recipients but said many other states had not done nearly as much.

The new report, to be released today by the Chapin Hall Center, followed 1,075 parents, mainly black single mothers, who applied in Milwaukee in 1999 to the Temporary Assistance to Needy Families program, the new name for welfare adopted by Congress in 1996. Most of those women cycled into and out of the program in subsequent years, some working intermittently.

But four years after they first contacted the welfare agency, only one-third of the parents held jobs in each quarter of 2003. Few, even among the successful workers, received enough income through work and public benefits to lift them above the poverty line.

"Most of these TANF applicants were no better off, and in many cases they were worse off than when they

Studies that followed Congress's action found that large numbers of single mothers around the country did enter the work force, though few escaped poverty. One of the most visible changes was a huge drop in the number of welfare recipients, by more than half nationally and by 80 percent in Wisconsin.

The rolls shrank in part because some mothers entering welfare were more quickly ushered into jobs, but at least half the decline reflected a drop in first-time applicants, said Steven J. Haider, an economist at the University of Michigan.

Scholars attribute the decline in applications to several factors, including a wider availability of low-end jobs, new supports like the earned-income tax credit and a deterrent effect of more stringent welfare rules.

This year Congress acted to stiffen work requirements more, penalizing states that did not increase the share of welfare recipients going into jobs or into preparation for employment. Some experts say this mandate may be unrealistic, given the traits of the remaining welfare population.

Experts said they were startled by the high proportion of welfare applicants in Milwaukee who had come to the attention of child welfare officials: in a five-year period, 40 percent of the parents were investigated for the possibility of abuse or neglect, and a child had been removed from the homes of 16 percent.

Since most of these parents had already been investigated, the study did not indicate that the welfare program itself, with its required work or training efforts, was causing child abuse. But at the least, Dr. Courtney said, the findings show that many parents seeking welfare are having "a profound difficulty balancing the demands of work and parenting."

"The population that remains is, on average, a much needier population, and they were not helped."

sity of Chicago, said that in addition to helping applicants with job skills, welfare agencies must more aggressively address personal and family problems.

Wisconsin had already recognized this challenge when the study was under way and has taken steps to coordinate child welfare and other services with the jobs program, said Jennifer L. Noyes, who ran the state's revamped welfare agency in 2000 and 2001 and is now a researcher at the University of Wisconsin.

"The program hasn't been static," Ms. Noyes said. "It is constantly changing in response to needs."

In a written statement, Roberta Gassman, Wisconsin's secretary of workforce development, called the new study important and said it showed the

sought assistance," Dr. Courtney wrote with his co-author, Amy Dworsky, a researcher at the Chapin Hall Center.

Under Gov. Tommy G. Thompson, Wisconsin led the way in welfare reform in the 1990's, pushing many applicants quickly into jobs or community service work and providing supports including supplements to the federal earned-income tax credit and wider access to Medicaid. Wisconsin also passed along fathers' child support payments to mothers, contrary to states' common practice of keeping them to offset welfare costs.

In 1996, Congress adopted similar goals for the nation, though Wisconsin has remained a showcase because of its strong work requirements for those deemed able.

■ **Correction:** May 18, 2006. An article yesterday about Wisconsin's welfare-to-work system misstated the university affiliation of Steven J. Haider, who described the national decline in welfare applicants. He is an economist at Michigan State University, not the University of Michigan.

New Rules Will Require States to Move Welfare Recipients to Work

By Robert Pear
June 28, 2006

The Bush administration plans to issue sweeping new rules on Wednesday that will require states to move much larger numbers of poor people from welfare to work.

The rules, drafted in response to a budget signed into law by President Bush in February, represent the biggest changes in welfare policy since 1996, when Congress abolished the federal guarantee of cash assistance for the nation's poorest children.

Since then, the number of welfare recipients has plunged more than 60 percent, to 4.4 million people, from 12.2 million. Most of the decline occurred in the first years, before the 2001 recession. Federal and state officials say they expect the new rules to speed the decline in welfare rolls, which has slowed in recent years.

The rules are far more than a bureaucratic application of the new law, passed after four years of partisan deadlock. For the first time, they set a uniform definition for permissible work activities and require states to verify and document the number of hours worked by welfare recipients.

Nationally, in 2004, the last year for which official figures are available, about 32 percent of adults on welfare were working. Under the new rules, 50 percent of adult welfare recipients must be engaged in work or training in the fiscal year that starts Oct. 1, or states will face financial penalties. The penalties can reduce a state's federal welfare grant by 5 percent in the first year and by two additional percentage points for each subsequent year of noncompliance, up to a maximum penalty of 21 percent.

Some state officials and antipoverty groups, including many who opposed the 1996 law, say the new work requirements are unrealistic. But Bush administration officials point to Georgia as evidence that the goals are achievable.

Gov. Sonny Perdue of Georgia, a Republican, said 69 percent of his state's adult welfare recipients were either working or in work-training programs, up from 8 percent four years ago. Moreover, Mr. Perdue said, the number of adult welfare cases has declined to 8,100, from 30,590 in 2002. In 32 of Georgia's 159 counties, he said, all the adults on welfare are employed or in training programs.

Members of Congress thought they were setting stringent work requirements when they created the current welfare program, Temporary Assistance for Needy Families, in 1996. But state officials quickly discovered that the requirements were much less onerous than they had thought.

Under the old law, the work requirements were reduced whenever states reduced the number of families on welfare, compared with the 1995 level. In theory, 50 percent of adult welfare recipients were supposed to be working. But if a state's caseload dropped 45 percent, the work requirement was slashed by 45 percentage points, so that only 5 percent of the state's welfare recipients had to be working.

> *"Welfare" used to mean a monthly check that could be immediately converted to cash. But more than half of the money now goes into child care, education, training and other services.*

Wade F. Horn, an assistant secretary of health and human services, said this provision of the 1996 law, known as a "caseload reduction credit," had wiped out any meaningful work requirements. Under the new rules, states will receive credit only for future reductions in their welfare rolls. The base year, for the purpose of comparison, will be 2005.

The new requirements may come as a shock to many states. In 2004, all states but Indiana and Mississippi met their work participation requirements, as calculated by the federal government. In 19 states, the required work participation rate—after taking account of steep declines in the welfare rolls—was zero.

The administration has scheduled a news conference for Wednesday to announce the rules, which, under the new law, must be issued by the end of this month.

Crystal A. Robinson, a 26-year-old mother of three in Minneapolis, said she believed that stricter work requirements could be helpful if states provided generous subsidies for child care.

Ms. Robinson received cash assistance from 2000 to 2002 and now receives help with her child care costs.

"I found a job I liked," said Ms. Robinson, who works 40 hours a week at a local hospital. "I'm a very hard worker.

But the child care would be unaffordable without assistance from Hennepin County."

Another welfare recipient, Laura L. Kegerreis, 33, receives $497 a month for herself and her three children while she takes job-preparation courses at Harrisburg Area Community College in Pennsylvania. M[s]. Kegerreis said the new work requirements could force her to take fewer classes, prolonging her stay on welfare and delaying her ability to get a professional credential.

The new law reauthorizes welfare programs through September 2010. The basic federal block grant remains $16.5 billion a year and is not adjusted for inflation or changes in the number of people on the rolls.

"Welfare" used to mean a monthly check that could be immediately converted to cash. But more than half of the money now goes into child care, education, training and other services—a huge shift since 1996.

Under the new rules, the federal government will spend $150 million a year on programs to help couples form "healthy marriages." Up to $50 million of this amount can be spent on activities promoting "responsible fatherhood." These activities could include seminars on the causes of domestic violence and child abuse.

After President Bill Clinton signed the 1996 welfare law, he gave states a large amount of discretion, saying he trusted them to help families become self-sufficient. The new rules limit the flexibility that states were granted in 1996. They define 12 acceptable types of work activity, including subsidized and unsubsidized employment, community service, on-the-job training, job search (usually limited to six weeks a year) and vocational education training (up to 12 months in a lifetime).

Federal officials said they were adopting uniform standards because the definition of work now varied from state to state, and even from year to year within the same state. As a result, they said, it is difficult to compare states' performance.

Today, as in 1996, many Democrats say the welfare law creates a perverse incentive. A state can comply by putting some people to work and by simply removing others from the rolls, regardless of whether they find jobs.

In an executive order on Friday, Gov. John Lynch of New Hampshire, a Democrat, made clear that he wanted to meet the federal requirements not just by closing cases, but by moving people to "lasting employment and self-sufficiency." Mr. Lynch said he intended to increase child care, transportation, education and other services to help people stay off welfare.

States could avoid many restrictions of the 1996 law by providing assistance entirely with state money, through separate state programs.

A Welfare Law Milestone Finds Many Left Behind

By Erik Eckholm
August 22, 2006

Over the last five years, Mysheda Autry has received welfare checks and food stamps, gone through a welfare-to-work program and briefly held several jobs. She has also given birth to her second and third children.

Ms. Autry, 25, with a 10th-grade education, was finally overwhelmed by the demands of work and family, and in February she showed up at the People's Emergency Center, a social service agency, with her three children, a fourth on the way, no job and no place to live.

She has exceeded the usual five-year limit for receiving welfare, and although the state has given her a reprieve, her benefits will be cut off,

she has been warned, if she does not resume full-time job-skill classes and a job search within eight and a half months after her new baby is born.

As political leaders give two cheers on Tuesday for the 10th anniversary of the welfare reform law that helped draw many single mothers from dependency into the work force, though often leaving them still in poverty, social workers and researchers are raising concerns about families that have not made the transition and often lead extraordinarily precarious lives.

These include mothers who, so beleaguered by personal problems and parenting that they have not been able to keep jobs, continue to need counsel-

ing and cash. They also include another large group of poor mothers—one million by some estimates—who are neither working nor receiving benefits.

The central idea of the nation's public assistance programs since 1996 has been that cash aid should be only a temporary support while parents are ushered into jobs, with skills training and child-care subsidies to help. The federal government set a time limit of five years for individual recipients, though exemptions were allowed for hardship cases, and states could extend aid with their own money.

Simply cutting families off at an arbitrary date has often proved impractical, because a significant group of mothers like Ms. Autry—no one has precise numbers—have not been able to hold on to jobs, even after attending required classes and while receiving other aid.

Their lives are simply too troubled by disabilities, turmoil and, often, bad are helped by food stamps, their children are often growing up in the poverty and tumult that the reforms were intended to end.

On Friday, days before her new baby was due, Ms. Autry described her life's obstacles so far.

Families that have not made the transition often lead extraordinarily precarious lives.

personal choices, researchers say. Poor education, lack of support from their families or their children's fathers, mental health and drug problems, and unstable living conditions are common among this group, and a rigid time limit may only harm the children.

"There aren't so many mothers who could never get on track, but getting them into work will take a lot more time and resources than many states have been able to provide," said La-Donna A. Pavetti, a welfare researcher with Mathematica Policy Research.

Without such extra attention, more will join a growing group of poor families, known to scholars as the "disconnected," that are scraping by without either cash benefits or employment.

According to new calculations by the private Center on Budget and Policy Priorities, as of 2003, the last year for which detailed data are available, about one million single mothers were neither working nor receiving cash benefits from welfare, disability or unemployment insurance and were not living with a partner who had any of these income sources either.

Other studies suggest that 10 percent to 20 percent of mothers who left the welfare rolls in the years after the 1996 overhaul did not have work or other significant means of support a year or two later.

While some have sources of unreported income—a little money from a new companion, perhaps—and many

She, five brothers and a sister grew up with a mother who split from Ms. Autry's father early on and was on welfare. After Ms. Autry became pregnant in the 10th grade and dropped out of school, she continued living in a crowded, tumultuous house filling with babies. She had to move out last February, however, when her mother moved to a smaller home that she now shares with two sons, the other daughter and that daughter's two children.

The father of Ms. Autry's 6-year-old boy is out of the picture, as is the father of the girl whose birth is imminent. The father of her 3-year-old girl and her 21-month-old boy is in prison.

After the birth of her first child, she worked at McDonald's for several months. But she could not stand it, she said, when the boy started referring to her mother as Mom.

She went into a jobs program, working 20 hours a week at a Y.M.C.A. with her wages paid by the welfare office and spending an additional 10 hours a week in a required search for permanent work. Eventually she landed a receptionist's job at a construction company where she worked for seven months.

"I just couldn't manage the child care," she said, though the state offered aid. At the time, her mother, who had been the prime caregiver, had herself been required to go into a work program.

For the last two years, Ms. Autry has received cash welfare benefits of $496 a month, plus $397 in food stamps. She has vowed to have no more children and to get her G.E.D. With no apparent drug or alcohol problem or serious cognitive drawbacks, she is in a better state than some other women lagging on welfare.

"We see families coming in who don't have one monolithic problem; instead it's a lethal combination of 10 issues in their lives that come together," said Gloria M. Guard, president of the People's Emergency Center, where Ms. Autry and her children found shelter. "They end up with lots of kids, no family support, no education, no coping skills, so they get a job and lose it and get another job and lose it. It's not like they are lying around not doing anything: their lives are constantly on the go as they run behind their kids. But they end up falling way behind."

Pennsylvania has been among the more generous states, Ms. Guard said, in allowing exemptions from time limits and working with mothers who show a willingness to try. But the services to help such women have been hurt by federal budget cuts, she said, and welfare agencies are under new federal pressure to get more women into jobs.

Ms. Autry and her children are living in a one-room "transitional apartment" at the emergency center. She may soon move into a larger efficiency apartment within the graduated system of the center, where, contrary to her current circumstances, she will have to shop and cook for herself and get the children to school or the doctor on her own—practice for a bigger move.

"Sooner or later she'll have to get a job," Ms. Guard said.

A possibility, once Ms. Autry gets some training, may be work as a home health aide.

But "the real problem," Ms. Guard said, "is how is she going to keep it."

IV. PERSPECTIVES ON CRIMINAL JUSTICE AND OFFENDER RE-ENTRY

The most recent information from the Bureau of Justice Statistics (2004) reports that there are more than 2.1 million offenders incarcerated, almost 7 million under correctional supervision in the United States, and more than 600,000 jail and prison inmates are released each year. How society chooses to help, or hinder, the re-entry of this population impacts every layer of society. Ex-judge Roland Amundson presents a unique perspective on the failure to rehabilitate offenders in the first article, and the special needs of juvenile offenders are addressed in the second. Nothing has a higher social cost than recidivism, yet it is unclear that government policies are designed to reduce this all-too-common eventuality. Re-entry is possible with help, as the third article suggests, but are we willing to provide the help that is needed? The fourth article discusses the conclusions of a special commission in New York that studied this issue. They propose significant new legislation to assist ex-offenders. Would it be wise to implement these changes nationwide?

As you read the following articles, consider how you would answer these questions.

14. A Fallen Judge Rethinks Crime and Punishment (01/13/06)

- What purpose would Amundson like to his example to promote?
- Why does Amundson call prison "warehousing?"

15. Redefining Juvenile Criminals (04/02/06)

- How do the services provided to juvenile offenders differ from those provided to adults?
- Should young people be subject to adult consequences for their actions?

16. NYC: A Fresh Start Needs Hands Willing to Help (06/13/06)

- What helps re-entry more than money for college?
- How did Randy A. Daniels treat Marc La Cloche inhumanely?

17. When "Help Wanted" Comes with a Catch: "Re-Entry" Is Often Grueling for Ex-Cons, Despite Laws and Programs to Aid Them (09/17/06)

- Why are existing laws inadequate to help ex-offenders find employment?
- What new laws are proposed in New York to assist re-entry?

A Fallen Judge Rethinks Crime and Punishment

By Kate Zernike
January 13, 2006

His last night behind bars, Roland Amundson was sitting in the prison library when he felt the large shadow of someone standing over him. He looked up to see the inmate others feared the most, a former motorcycle gang leader who had been convicted of killing a man in a bar fight—a murder so violent the court doubled the standard sentence.

The man wanted to talk.

Mr. Amundson had been the appellate judge who upheld that unusually strict sentence. Now, he was just a fellow prisoner, inmate No. 209383. "He asked if I remembered him," Mr. Amundson recalled in an interview in December. "He wanted me to know he didn't hold any hard feelings against me."

The encounter in October, Mr. Amundson said, was one of a dozen times in his three and a half years in prison that he was confronted by inmates whose sentences he had ordered or upheld in 15 years as a judge. Those experiences and Mr. Amundson's other dealings as a convicted felon—at his sentencing, prosecutors turned the

on charitable boards in Minneapolis, and seemed to know everyone. Colleagues described him as brilliant and charming.

Then he was caught taking $400,000 from a trust fund he oversaw for a woman with the mental capacity of a 3-year-old, money he spent on marble floors and a piano for his house as well as model trains, sculpture and china service for 80, all bought on eBay.

Now, serving the last months of his sentence in a halfway house here, Mr. Amundson is engaged in an uneasy and humbling round of self-reflection, examining the criminal justice system from a rare two-sided perspective while busying himself with a menial vocation: shoveling snow and taking orders to the printer for a sewing machine company he represented long ago as a lawyer.

"Judges can say they have no idea what's going on in prison," Mr. Amundson said from a worn couch in the halfway house. "But if you know what's going on and you are still callous, God help you. If you are part of the system that does the things the system can do, God help you."

hurt find unconvincing. "I don't think he feels like he did anything wrong," said Karen Dove, a guardian for Mr. Amundson's victim.

Prosecutors say they are skeptical that Mr. Amundson has learned much in prison; he has continued, they say, to expect special treatment. At one point, he tried to get into a boot camp program that would have halved his sentence; prosecutors blocked the move, saying it was intended for inmates with drug problems or illiteracy.

More recently, Mr. Amundson raised eyebrows with a Christmas card featuring an unshackled ball and chain. It included quotes from Dostoyevsky and Solzhenitsyn about the redemptive value of prison, as well as a picture of Mr. Amundson with his four young sons—reminding some of his critics of how many lives he has hurt.

"It was another indication that he hasn't seen the light," Ms. Dove said.

But relentlessly cheerful—"Come into my chambers," he greeted a visitor, his arm surveying his small cubicle with a leather chair jammed into the corner at the sewing company in nearby Eden Prairie—Mr. Amundson said he wants to use his experience to promote the importance of rehabilitation in prison.

After a boom in prison populations, there are now a record number of ex-felons getting out of prison each year—about 640,000 a year, up about 40 percent over the last decade—and more than half of them end up back there. Across the country, officials are experimenting with ways to smooth re-entry and prevent recidivism, with drug treatment or job training.

Mr. Amundson could get out 23 months early, in April, because of good behavior. He has surrendered his law license, and with few prospects for the future, says he wants to create homes for men coming out of prison, giving

"At 34, he is completely incapable of living in society. He's been raised by corrections officers."

words of his rulings against him to justify a longer term—have shaken the world view of a man who, from the bench, thought he knew all there was to know about crime and punishment.

Until 2001, Mr. Amundson, who is 56, was a highly regarded judge who sat on the Minnesota Court of Appeals, the state's second-highest court. Mentioned in legal circles as a likely nominee to the State Supreme Court, he was a popular public speaker, served

Like Sol Wachtler, the former chief judge of the New York State Court of Appeals who pleaded guilty in a harassment case and spent 13 months in federal prison in the early 1990's, Mr. Amundson belongs to a small group of distinguished jurists undone by the laws they had been sworn to uphold, who later came to claim redemption in their undoing.

In Mr. Amundson's case, it is a transformation that some people he

them a place to live and help with other hurdles to successful re-entry.

As a judge, Mr. Amundson says he had not thought about sentencing beyond his court; he has come to see its consequences from fellow inmates.

"I knew the era of rehabilitation was over, but I had no idea we had reduced it to just warehousing, and I don't think most judges do," he said.

Mr. Amundson recalled one man he met in prison who had been convicted of killing his parents after they abused him. At 18, he was sentenced to 18 years.

"At 34, he is completely incapable of living in society," Mr. Amundson said. "He's been raised by corrections officers."

Mr. Amundson, who is openly gay, continues to struggle with the court system in a custody battle with his former partner over their four adopted sons from Russia. He grew bitter about prison restrictions on communicating with the boys. What determines successful re-entry into society, he said, is family support.

"If there is any collection of men who need fathers more than the men in prison, I don't know it," he said. "You're dealing with men who need fathers and yet you're decimating their relationships with their children."

By the time he began adopting children in 1998, Mr. Amundson had been stealing for at least three years. He had set up a trust in the early 1990's for the mentally retarded daughter of a wealthy beer distributor he knew from his days representing the state's beer wholesalers. When the man died, Mr. Amundson became sole trustee.

He recalls putting his hand in his desk drawer and pulling out the first of 85 checks he forged. "It was like somebody else was doing it," he said.

Ms. Dove and another woman who worked for the retarded woman, now in her 30's, became suspicious in 2001 when they asked Mr. Amundson for money for a new roof on the woman's house, and he said the trust was empty. It had been worth more than $600,000 when the father's estate was settled seven years earlier.

In retrospect, Mr. Amundson says he wanted to be caught.

"I was tired of being Rolly Amundson, tired of being at everybody's beck and call, just tired," he said. "This was my vehicle to end it all."

Amy Klobuchar, the Hennepin County attorney, saw it in simpler terms. "I believe he was greedy and wanted to live a lifestyle that he didn't have the money to live," she said in December.

Mr. Amundson resigned as a judge and agreed to plead guilty, but he haggled over sentencing, she said, trying to avoid prison time. He sought to mitigate his sentence in 2002 by arguing that he suffered from bipolar disorder, but prosecutors pointed out that he had written an opinion rejecting psychological factors as mitigating. They sought a sentence 12 months longer than the guidelines recommended; Judge Amundson himself, they noted, had written opinions upholding extended sentences in cases where the victim was particularly vulnerable.

The judge sentenced Mr. Amundson to 69 months, as prosecutors requested, saying he had been drunk on power, and had acted not out of depression but out of a sense of entitlement. Mr. Amundson called in a long line of prominent witnesses—his pastor, a former Miss America, a former ambassador—to argue against a harsh sentence.

For her part, Ms. Klobuchar had what she recalled as "her guardian angels," two black defendants who happened onto the courtroom after they appeared in court on drug charges, and sat in the front row expressing their outrage as Mr. Amundson's friends testified.

"I don't think he should be treated any differently than the people that have walked through his own courtroom," she said.

Redefining Juvenile Criminals

By Avi Salzman
April 2, 2006

The envelope carrying the letter Katharine Czajka sent to her parents from the York Correctional Institution in Niantic was decorated with childish doodles and song lyrics, and was sealed "with a kiss." The markings would not have been out of place in the margins of a bored high school student's social studies notebook. But to Katharine's mother, Joanne Davidson of New Milford, they felt grossly out of place stamped with a return address from an adult prison.

"This is what she sends me on every envelope," Ms. Davidson said in a recent interview at a diner near her Danbury office. "She's a kid."

To Ms. Davidson, Katharine, who is 17, may be a child, but to Connecticut's Department of Correction she is an adult who faces adult charges of burglary, larceny and stealing her mother's car. Connecticut is one of three states where people as young as 16 are automatically charged as adults. The others are New York and North Carolina. In most states, those under 18 are sent to juvenile detention and receive services targeted to juveniles. In some states, the cutoff age is 17.

A bill being considered in the General Assembly seeks to change the law so that 16- and 17-year-olds are treated as juveniles as long as their crimes are not so serious as to merit stricter punishment. It passed through the Judiciary Committee on a 28 to 12 vote on Monday and was sent to the Appropriations Committee for another vote.

"We need to change the way we address services for youth," said State Representative Toni E. Walker, a Democrat from New Haven, who pushed the bill through the Judiciary Committee. "The State of Connecticut, if we don't watch out, will be parents to a lot of kids through the correctional system."

But the bill has encountered opposition in the criminal justice system, with Chief State's Attorney Christopher L. Morano calling it "disastrous for the people, for the public safety of the state, for the juveniles that would be part of the court, and for the system in general" in testimony before the Judiciary Committee last month.

Cost is also a concern for some of the bill's opponents. A report for the Legislature, released by a state panel in February 2004, found that raising the age of adult jurisdiction would cost nearly $84 million in operating expenses and $81 million in construction expenses. The Judicial Branch is currently updating those estimates.

The law's proponents argue that continuing to house 16- and 17-year-olds in adult prisons will cost the state more in the long run and turn troubled teenagers into hardened criminals. Some community activists hope changing the law can spur the state to reform the entire juvenile justice system, making it more community-based and emphasizing prevention over punishment.

Raising the age would certainly force a drastic shift in the way the state provides services to 16- and 17-year-olds accused or convicted of crimes. In the 2004–5 fiscal year, 15,600 children through the age of 15 went through the juvenile court system, while 13,218 16- and 17-year-olds were sent to adult criminal court. Adding thousands of people to the juvenile court system

would mean a huge shift in state resources, state officials said.

Proponents of the bill contend that the current system does not serve young people well. Those who are 16 or 17 are sent to prisons instead of juvenile detention centers, even while awaiting trial. Boys are sent to the John R. Manson Youth Institution in Cheshire, which houses 14- to 20-year-old inmates. As of March 1, there were 670 inmates at Manson.

> "You're taking them at an age when social learning is at its peak, and you're putting them in an adult detention system, where they have to soak up the culture to survive."

Manson was in the news last year after David Burgos, 17, who was being held on a probation violation, hanged himself with a sheet there in July. His mother, Diana Gonzalez of Bristol, said that she had trouble getting any information about her son while he was locked up—she did not visit him during the four months he was at Manson—and that he was not getting the services he needed for his bipolar disorder, attention deficit hyperactivity disorder and depression. Ms. Gonzalez testified in favor of raising the age before the Judiciary Committee last month.

"You take a kid with these problems and lock him up and see what it's going to do to him," she said in a recent interview.

As with every prison suicide, the Department of Correction is investigating Mr. Burgos's death, and a spokeswoman would not comment on specifics of his case.

The Niantic prison is the state's only women's prison, and young offenders like Katharine Czajka are held in a separate area from adults. Niantic had 1,290 inmates as of March 1, and 27 of them were 18 or younger. Ms. Davidson, Katharine's mother, said she was concerned that her daughter was interacting with older inmates at meals, in vans on the way to court, and when

she went to get medicine. She also complained that her daughter was not placed in prison high school classes for four weeks.

Stacy Smith, a spokeswoman for the Department of Correction, said officers accompany younger inmates whenever they are near the adults.

Sometimes the prison classes have a waiting list, but inmates will then receive educational materials in their cells, Ms. Smith said. Ms. Davidson said her daughter did not receive the materials during the four weeks she was waiting to enroll. Katharine was eventually transferred to a drug treatment program in Bridgeport, but walked out, Ms. Davidson said. She said last week that there was a warrant out for Katharine's arrest.

Juveniles receive more services than adults throughout the criminal justice process. For instance, juveniles are given a probation officer to determine what services they need when they first go to court. On the adult side, people charged with crimes are not assigned probation officers until they are sentenced. And probation officers on the juvenile side are able to devote more time to each case, said Deborah J. Fuller, the director of external affairs for the Judicial Branch. The average caseload for a juvenile probation officer is 54 cases, while adult probation officers handle 125, according to the Judicial Branch.

"The thing that makes juvenile unique is that it has a much higher service level," Ms. Fuller said.

Ann-Marie DeGraffenreidt, a lawyer at the nonprofit Center for Children's Advocacy in Hartford, which represents poor children, said she thought the juvenile court system offered more flexibility than criminal court. Police officers deal with the two categories of offenders differently. One 16-year-old girl she represented was arrested for making prank phone calls and placed in jail overnight, Ms. DeGraffenreidt said. If the girl had been 15, Ms. DeGraffenreidt said, the officer would have given her a summons to appear in juvenile court and let her go.

"The response is different from the initial response all the way through," she said. "The perspective of the two courts is different, in that adult court is focused on punishment for crime as opposed to rehabilitation. The philosophy behind juvenile court is that kids aren't set in stone."

Young people should not be subject to adult consequences for childish acts, said Abby Anderson, senior policy associate for the Connecticut Juvenile Justice Alliance, a nonprofit advocacy organization in Bridgeport.

"It doesn't matter what you do, you're an adult," she said. "If you get caught drinking at a football game, if there's a fight in the hall."

The bill's proponents said they have science on their side. The brains of 16- and 17-year-olds are not fully developed, said Dr. Abigail Baird, a professor in Department of Psychological and Brain Sciences at Dartmouth. That doesn't mean that they cannot distinguish between right and wrong, Dr. Baird said, but it does create problems when they are placed in prison with more-mature adults.

"You're taking them at an age when social learning is at its peak, and you're putting them in an adult detention system, where they have to soak up the culture to survive," she said.

That is one reason some researchers said that adolescents placed in prison with adults are more likely to commit crimes when they are released. Dr. Donna M. Bishop, a professor of criminal justice at Northeastern University in Boston, researched the difference in recidivism rates among more than 5,000 teenagers in Florida, half of whom were treated as juveniles and half of whom were treated as adults for similar crimes. In Florida, prosecutors

have wide discretion over how to try juveniles. Dr. Bishop found that about 19 percent of those treated as juveniles committed new crimes, while about 31 percent of those tried as adults broke the law again.

When they were placed in the adult system, young people "were more likely to reoffend, reoffended more quickly, and reoffended at higher rates," she said.

But not everyone is convinced that taking 16- and 17-year-olds out of the adult system would make Connecticut safer. The bill has drawn opposition from some of the people who deal most closely with 16- and 17-year-old offenders.

Mr. Morano, the chief state's attorney, said in his testimony that there was no valid reason to change the law and that the state does not have the resources to support an influx of thousands of new juveniles. He also said that a recent spike in youth violence in Connecticut's cities has alarmed him, convincing him that the state needs to have accountability as soon as possible.

"I'm seeing violence that is coming from people who are of a younger and younger age," he said in the testimony.

Advocates of the bill noted that violent crime committed by juveniles has decreased since the mid-1990's, when it peaked, according to statistics compiled through 2003 by the Office of Juvenile Justice and Delinquency Prevention, which is part of the federal Justice Department.

The Connecticut Police Chiefs Association also expressed concern to the Judiciary Committee about the bill. Chief James Strillacci of West Hartford, speaking for the organization, said changing the law would complicate the jobs of police officers. When they question a juvenile, officers need to make sure a parent is present, Chief Strillacci said. Because 16- and 17-year-olds can drive, police officers need to be able to question them in the case of a car accident without having to wait for their parents to arrive.

"What do we do in the case of a motor vehicle accident?" he said in an interview last week. "Are we going to be able to do our jobs?"

In addition, the police already struggle to find room in juvenile detention for young people who have broken the law, Chief Strillacci said. Sometimes, officers have to let offenders go because detention centers are full.

"If there's not a place to put them, we have to turn them loose," he said. "We're concerned that will happen more often."

The law's advocates acknowledge that the state's juvenile system is strained and may not be able to absorb more children. That is why some proponents want to shift the emphasis in juvenile justice from state institutions to community-based programs. Community members in Hartford started a Juvenile Review Board last year that some lawmakers said they thought could be a model for other big cities in Connecticut. The board—made up of representatives from the police, schools, the religious community, child welfare and mental health services and other community agencies—evaluates juvenile offenders.

The emphasis is on rehabilitating children and finding the services they and their parents need, said Merva Jackson, a community activist who helped set up the program. The children will still need to make up for their mistakes—by fixing property they vandalized and meeting with mentors, for instance—and will be sent to the juvenile court if they do not comply.

Gov. M. Jodi Rell has placed $550,000 in the proposed budget for next fiscal year to pay for the Hartford board and set up new boards in New Haven and Bridgeport. Ms. Jackson acknowledged that it would be expensive to replicate Hartford's model throughout the state, but cautioned against doing nothing.

"How much does it cost to lock them up at 16 anyway?" she asked. "You kill them. You kill their spirit."

NYC: A Fresh Start Needs Hands Willing to Help

By Clyde Haberman
June 13, 2006

Gregory Pereira had plenty of drug convictions and the prison sentences that went with them. They were usually short stretches—a year here, 18 months there—and they finally got Mr. Pereira to realize that life on New York's margins had not worked out. "I wasn't," he said with ample understatement, "that good a criminal."

He turned his life around. First, he managed to stay out of prison. Eventually, he kicked his drug habit. He went to school and earned a bachelor's degree. "I don't know if I had a spiritual awakening or reckoning or what," Mr. Pereira said, "but I realized I had to give something back."

He began to do just that. He managed H.I.V.-prevention programs. And he continued his studies. Now 46, he is getting a master's degree in public administration from Metropolitan College of New York, on Varick Street, where the students are typically well above traditional college age.

There are many ways Mr. Pereira could have taken note of this latest passage. He chose to celebrate the other evening with a dozen men and women who are also receiving degrees this

forget that some are no longer bad guys. They seek redemption. But maybe they need a hand to find it.

Mr. Pereira did. So did the other onetime inmates gathered with him in celebration in an auditorium of the City University Graduate Center.

All belonged to a program called College and Community Fellowship, created six years ago to help former inmates pursue college studies, in most cases while they also hold full-time jobs. More than 100 people have taken part so far. At some point along the way, all had been written off as hopeless lowlifes, even no-lifes. Now they are graduating from college, some with advanced degrees.

And not one, the sponsors say, has landed back in jail.

Participants receive some cash, $600 a semester, to ease the pain of tuition a bit. Perhaps more important, they get mentoring and encouragement and, as the program's name says, fellowship.

"The money helps, but it's really the camaraderie and the hope," said Aracelis Turino, who did 10 years in federal prisons on a drug-related conviction. At 37, she is getting her bachelor's degree

a helping hand should be self-evident. Every now and then, though, a situation comes along to bring the point home.

A good example is the case of a man named Marc La Cloche. He appeared in this column more than once. Mr. La Cloche was a Bronx man who, during an 11-year stretch in New York prisons for first-degree robbery, learned to be a barber. He loved cutting hair. After he was freed in 2001, he sought the state license required to pursue his new craft.

Time and again, the office of New York's secretary of state, Randy A. Daniels, made sure that he didn't succeed. His criminal past, state officials said, proved that he lacked the "good moral character" to be a barber. Ultimately, Mr. La Cloche was beaten down. He died last October at 40, a lonely man not given a shot.

In his attempt to get a license, he had taken Mr. Daniels to court. When Mr. La Cloche died, so did his case. Justice Louis B. York of State Supreme Court in Manhattan signed a formal dismissal order on June 1. But in his ruling the judge did not hide his "outrage and despair" over what the state officials had done, over "the inhumanity exhibited by human beings with power over one person without power."

At least Mr. Pereira, Ms. Turino and the others got a chance to start over. So they celebrated together at the Graduate Center. They heard speeches of encouragement, and they performed a short play of their own about life behind bars and, more hopefully, the road ahead.

There was a printed program for the evening, designed by Mr. Pereira. Its dominating feature was an illustration of a phoenix.

> *At some point along the way, all had been written off as hopeless lowlifes, even no-lifes. Now they are graduating from college.*

spring from colleges in the city and its suburbs. They had that achievement in common. That, and one other thing:

They were all former convicts.

It is sometimes easy to forget, in this get-tough-on-crime era, that the bad guys eventually get out of prison, or most of them anyway. It is even easier to

in social work from Lehman College, in the Bronx. "We sit together," Ms. Turino said, "and discuss who's having issues, and the barriers we all face, and the stigmas."

For sure, this is not the only program in the city for onetime criminals ready to change their lives. The need for such

When "Help Wanted" Comes with a Catch: "Re-Entry" Is Often Grueling for Ex-Cons, Despite Laws and Programs to Aid Them

By Joseph P. Fried
September 17, 2006

After four years in prison for a robbery conviction, Christopher Ortiz says, he spent nearly two years being rejected for one unskilled job after another. Finally, a few months ago, he landed work handling stock at a food company.

Mr. Ortiz, a 24-year-old Bronx resident, said he believed that his criminal record was the reason for the rejections, including 20 by companies that interviewed him.

Tausha Haynes, 29, of Syracuse did not get jail terms for her guilty pleas to petty larceny in two cases and to disorderly conduct in a third. But her effort to turn her life around by becoming a licensed practical nurse has been stymied by her criminal record—and inaccuracies that made it look even worse, according to Ms. Haynes and a group that is helping her correct the record.

Mr. Ortiz's and Ms. Haynes's stories are hardly unusual. And rehabilitation

the mid-90's, officials and politicians, even conservatives like President Bush, are stressing the need for rehabilitation programs, including those dealing with employment. The programs are now called re-entry more often than rehabilitation, as in re-entry to law-abiding society.

In that context, a report in May by a special committee of the New York State Bar Association said the state needed to do much more to reduce the major hurdles, in employment and other aspects of rehabilitation, that confront people with criminal records.

The Pataki administration's director of criminal justice, Chauncey G. Parker, said at a legislative hearing earlier this year that he was confident the administration's efforts "will be looked upon as a model for other states." He cited programs that included vocational training, access to education and drug abuse treatment.

people without criminal records still exists." It cited other research showing that up to 60 percent of former prisoners in the state are unemployed one year after release. More than 25,000 prisoners have been released annually from New York State prisons in recent years, and thousands more after serving sentences in local jails.

The panel noted that under state law, an applicant considered qualified to do a job cannot be refused employment based on a criminal conviction unless there is a "direct relationship" between the offense and the job, or unless hiring the ex-convict poses an "unreasonable risk" to property or safety. To make those determinations, the panel said, the law requires the employer to "engage in a balancing test," weighing factors like the job's specific duties, the applicant's age when the crime was committed and the time that has since elapsed.

An aversion to ex-convicts is not always the reason when employers violate that law, the panel added. Another concern for companies is that employers can be held liable for the criminal actions of their employees, under the theory of "negligent hiring," the report said.

In the belief that reducing the fear of liability will lead to more hiring of people with criminal records, the panel recommended two new laws.

One would provide that in a lawsuit for negligent hiring based on the action of a worker with a criminal history, a demonstration that an employer complied with the balancing test would strengthen its defense. Evidence of compliance could be a simple worksheet on which the company indicated

An inability to find a job is a reason that many people with criminal records get into further trouble.

experts say that an inability to find a job is a reason that many people with criminal records get into further trouble.

In the 1980's and 90's, as crime rates climbed sharply in the nation, rehabilitation often took a back seat as politicians and criminal-justice officials focused more on providing harsher sentencing than on cutting recidivism.

In the last few years, though, after a general drop in the crime rates since

But the panel of lawyers said wider-reaching state action was necessary. Its recommendations include making more effective a current state law prohibiting unwarranted discrimination against job applicants who have criminal records; people with such records and their advocates say many employers do not comply with that law.

The bar association panel said, "A demonstrated preference for hiring

how it had assessed the factors in the test, the panel's report said.

The other proposal would establish a state program to provide employers with bonding to cover the cost of liability for negligent hiring if they lost such lawsuits.

The report also called for a law giving released prisoners free copies of their criminal records, to check that the records are accurate. Too often they are not, defense lawyers say. People receiving nonprison sentences would get their records at sentencing.

Ms. Haynes, the Syracuse woman, said she suspected that her inaccurate record had played a role in her rejection by a hospital and a nursing home where she sought work as a licensed practical nurse after completing training for the work in June. "I did so well on the interviews," she said.

Alan Rosenthal, an official in the Syracuse office of the Center for Community Alternatives, which helps convicted people, said that in addition to Ms. Haynes's convictions for petty larceny and disorderly conduct, her record had entries for assault and weapons possession—which applied to another Syracuse woman with a similar name and date of birth. Whether Ms. Haynes would have been hired with an accurate record is not known, but the errors were an added strike against her, said Mr. Rosenthal, who was a member of the bar association panel that produced the report.

(The report, "Re-entry and Reintegration: The Road to Public Safety," is available at www.nysba.org through the "sections/committees" link to the Special Committee on Collateral Consequences of Criminal Proceedings.)

Reactions to the panel's recommendations varied among people who help those with criminal backgrounds find jobs.

Robert Carmona, president of Strive, a nonprofit group, called the recommendations "perfectly valid."

Peter Cove, founder of America Works, a private company, said that while job discrimination against people with criminal records existed, it was not the major issue. The biggest problem, he said, is that there are too few programs to help such people find work.

The panel's chairman, Peter J. W. Sherwin, a partner with the law firm of Proskauer Rose, said the bar association had not yet decided whether to adopt the report as its official position, but he said he thought the recommended steps "would make New York a better and safer place for all of us."

V. PERSPECTIVES ON IMMIGRATION REFORM

Immigration reform options dominated Washington news during most of the first half of 2006. President Bush's sympathy for immigrants, especially for those from Mexico, is well-rooted in his Texas experience according to the first article. The evidence in the second article seems to support the conclusion that immigrants assimilate economically by the second or third generation despite the legal obstacles to employment for the undocumented. The third article describes how easily the legal obstacles are avoided by both employer and undocumented employee, but it is easy to forget that immigration reform is not just about policies and border issues. The last article brings the personal to life. To one, the basement apartment is a "dungeon;" to another, it is "a better life for our children." Whose perspective is correct?

As you read the following articles, consider how you would answer these questions.

18. The Immigration Debate: The Context
Behind a Talk, Bush's History (05/16/06)

- What is President Bush's personal attitude toward Mexican immigrants?
- Why is President Bush getting tougher on border security?

19. Economic View: Immigration Math
It's a Long Story (06/18/06)

- What is "one of the paradoxes of Mexican immigration?"
- From a global perspective, what are the advantages of accepting immigrants?

20. Here Illegally, Working Hard and Paying Taxes (06/19/06)

- How hard is it to get forged papers in Minneapolis?
- What loophole helps employers hire undocumented immigrants?

21. On Lucille Avenue, the Immigration Debate (06/26/06)

- Why is Patrick Nicolosi so concerned about living close to illegal immigrants?
- Is the Escheverria family an example of why immigration is a problem, or an example of why immigrants are good for America?

The Immigration Debate: The Context
Behind a Talk, Bush's History

By Elisabeth Bumiller
May 16, 2006

The headline news from President Bush's immigration speech on Monday was troops to the border, but in substance and tone the address reflected the more subtle approach of a man shaped by Texas border-state politics and longtime personal views.

In an effort to placate conservatives, Mr. Bush talked tough about cracking down on immigrants who slip across the United States' long border with Mexico.

But the real theme of his speech was that the nation can be, as he phrased it, "a lawful society and a welcoming society at the same time" and that Congress could find a middle ground between deporting illegal immigrants and granting them immediate citizenship.

What was remarkable to people who knew Mr. Bush in Texas was how much he still believes in the power of immigration to invigorate the nation.

"He's always had a more welcoming attitude," said Bruce Buchanan, a

Democrats arrayed against him and with his own party so split on the issue.

It is also unclear if Congress can even enact an immigration bill this year when the Senate is pushing a temporary guest worker program and the House favors a harsher, enforcement-only approach. So far Mr. Bush, who insists he is not advocating amnesty, has spoken favorably of the Senate approach—a position consistent with his views in the past.

"He understands this community in the way you do when you live in a border state," said Israel Hernandez, an assistant secretary at the Commerce Department who traveled with Mr. Bush as a personal aide when he first ran for governor. "Philosophically, he understands why people want to come to the U.S. And he doesn't consider them a threat."

There were no major battles over immigration or immigration legislation when Mr. Bush was governor,

to be Texans," said Paul Burka, senior executive editor of Texas Monthly, who closely followed Mr. Bush then. "He didn't believe in closing the borders."

Mr. Bush first met Mexican immigrants at public school in Midland, Tex., where Hispanics made up 25 percent of the population. Later, when he owned a small, unsuccessful oil company, he employed Mexican immigrants in the fields. When he was the managing partner of the Texas Rangers, he reveled in going into the dugout and joking with the players, many of them Hispanic, in fractured Spanglish.

"In every dimension of his career, whether it was politics or the private sector or the sports world, he's been engaged with the Hispanic population," Mr. Hernandez said.

Mr. Bush was also living in a state that has stronger historical and cultural ties to Mexico than any other.

"The cultures mingled much more freely here than in California," Mr. Burka said. "Here there was not nearly as much antipathy. There were always workers coming over, and they were very essential."

At the same time, Karl Rove, Mr. Bush's veteran political adviser, recognized that there was potential in the Hispanic vote and that Republicans could appeal to them on abortion, religion and family values.

"Karl has always been a strong believer that Hispanics were a natural Republican constituency," Mr. Burka said. "He once told me that 'we have about 15 years to put this together.'" When Mr. Bush got to the White House, immigration was going to be a signature issue, a key to his relationship with President Vicente Fox of Mexico and essential in attracting Hispanic voters to a Republican Party that Mr. Rove envisioned as dominant for decades to come.

> ## *"They bring to America the values of faith in God, love of family, hard work and self-reliance."*

presidential scholar at the University of Texas. "He always spoke well of Mexican nationals and regarded them as hard-working people. So his grace notes on this subject are high."

Mr. Bush had three political goals in making the speech: appealing to the public's desire to see something done, mollifying an important part of his Republican base and shaping a compromise between competing immigration bills in the Senate and House. Republicans acknowledge that it will be difficult for Mr. Bush to reach these goals with

but he is remembered for saying emphatically that the children of illegal immigrants had a right to go to Texas schools. His views were in sharp contrast to those of another politician of the time, Pete Wilson, who closely tied his successful 1994 race for California governor to Proposition 187, a ballot initiative that denied public services to illegal immigrants and that passed overwhelmingly.

"There was never any effort to cut off benefits, and Bush basically bought into the notion that they were going

The Sept. 11 attacks suspended the push on the issue until late in the first term, but in a speech in January 2004 Mr. Bush threw himself into the subject with personal passion.

"As a Texan, I have known many immigrant families, mainly from Mexico, and I have seen what they add to our country," Mr. Bush told hundreds of wildly cheering Hispanics at a gathering in the East Room of the White House. "They bring to America the values of faith in God, love of family, hard work and self-reliance, the values that made us a great nation to begin with."

Every generation of immigrants, he added, "has reaffirmed the wisdom of remaining open to the talents and dreams of the world."

Mr. Bush's speech that day, more than 2,300 words, devoted only 200 of them to border security. Even then, he mentioned only what he said the nation was doing right—employing more Border Patrol agents and improving technology—and made no urgent statement, as he did Monday night, that "we do not yet have full control of the border."

In that same speech, Mr. Bush proposed a temporary guest worker program for the nation's 11 million or so illegal immigrants, as well as for immigrants seeking to enter the United States. The reaction was immediate and largely negative; immigrants and many Democrats said the plan did not go far enough, and conservatives said it amounted to amnesty.

Mr. Bush dropped the proposal as too risky for his 2004 re-election race, but he campaigned heavily among Hispanic constituencies and attracted 40 percent of the Hispanic vote.

With the election out of the way, Mr. Bush picked up the issue last October, but by then he had changed his emphasis to border security to calm conservatives. On Monday night, with his polls showing a drop in conservative support in part because of his immigration proposals, he toughened his language even more.

Now immigration, as divisive as it is, remains as Mr. Bush's last major domestic issue and a test of his remaining powers as president.

"He's putting capital behind it," said Mark McKinnon, the president's campaign media consultant. "It would be a lot easier just to let it go away."

Economic View: Immigration Math
It's a Long Story

By Daniel Altman
June 18, 2006

Much of today's debate about immigration revolves around the same old questions: How much do immigrants contribute to production? Do they take jobs away from people born in the United States? And what kinds of social services do they use? Yet every immigrant represents much more than just one worker or one potential citizen. To understand fully how immigration will shape the economy, you can't just look at one generation—you have to look into the future.

Sociologists and economists are just beginning to study the performance of second- and third-generation members of immigrant families. Because of the variety of experiences of people from different countries and cultures, it's not easy to generalize. But recent research has already uncovered some pertinent facts.

Education is a good place to start, because it's strongly correlated with future earnings. Children of immigrants complete more years of education than their native-born counterparts of similar socioeconomic backgrounds. "You can expect a child of immigrants whose parents have 10 years of education to do a lot better than a child of natives whose parents have 10 years of education," said David Card, a professor of economics at the University of California, Berkeley. Being a child of immigrants, he said, "sort of boosts your drive."

As a whole, though, the second generation also tends to move toward the American average, Professor Card said. Some graduate from high school even though their parents didn't, but some whose parents have doctorates will earn only bachelor's degrees.

Still, it can take several generations for poor immigrant families to catch up to American norms. "For the largest immigrant group—that is Mexicans and Mexican-Americans—the picture is progress, but still lagging behind other Americans," said Hans P. Johnson, a research fellow at the Public Policy Institute of California. "They're doing much better than their parents, graduating from high school, but they still have very low graduation rates from college."

But despite the lag in education, Mr. Johnson said, Mexican immigrants and their families don't have much trouble finding jobs. "One of the paradoxes of Mexican immigration is that you have these workers with low skills but incredibly high employment rates," he said. "The second generation isn't able to maintain employment levels that are quite so high, but they're basically in the same ballpark."

Second generations of immigrant families are managing to climb the skills ladder, too. A recent survey by the Census Bureau reveals that 40 percent of the female workers and 37 percent of the male workers in the second generation took professional or management positions, up from 30 and 24 percent, respectively, in the first generation. The survey, taken in 2004, included many adults whose parents came to the United States decades ago, noted William H. Frey, a visiting fellow at the Brookings Institution in Washington who compiled data from the survey. With more recent immigrants, he said, it's possible that lower education rates may eventually lead to worse outcomes.

Other factors could also make success more difficult for today's children of immigrants, compared with those of the past.

One is increased competition. The children of Italians and Poles who came to the United States around the turn of the 20th century didn't face much of it, because the government imposed quotas on immigration after their parents arrived, said Roger Waldinger, a professor of sociology at the University of California, Los Angeles. By contrast, the children of recent arrivals face competition from successive waves of immigrants from numerous regions.

Inequality of income and wealth is another factor that could affect opportunities. "The second generation of Italians and Poles came of age in an era of historically low inequality," Professor Waldinger said. "The second generation of Mexican immigrants is coming of age in an era of historically

high inequality, and that has to work to the disadvantage of those with low levels of schooling."

But there are also forces working in the opposite direction. For one thing, the children of today's immigrants will have much better access to education

Society is "much more open to outsiders" in top jobs and at elite colleges than it ever was before.

and the labor market than those of a century ago. "It almost certainly will be the case that tomorrow's third generation will have better outcomes than today's third generation," Mr. Johnson said. "The conditions today are better in terms of educational opportunities."

Adding to that, members of several immigrant groups have often risen quickly to—or even started at—the top of the wage scale. Professor Waldinger said that "the median for Indian immigrants is 16 years of schooling" and that, on balance, "the Indians, the Koreans, the Chinese—they're already successful." One reason, he added, is that society is "much more open to outsiders" in top jobs and at elite colleges than it ever was before.

Even if successive generations of immigrants manage to become as ec-

onomically successful as native-born Americans, a big question will remain: How many people do we really want in the United States? From the standpoint of government fiscal policy, Professor Card said, you could argue that the only immigrants you'd want in the United States were those "whose children are going to get Ph.D.'s" and would therefore be economically productive.

Some people might argue that a larger population raises housing prices and causes more pollution, he said. But there can be advantages to size, too. "If you have population growth, you can finance intergenerational transfer systems" like Social Security and Medicare, he said. And lest we forget, he said, "big countries have more power."

Mr. Frey agreed that waves of immigration could help to solidify a country's position in the world. In that respect, he said, Europe and Japan have a problem. "They have a very aging society because they don't like immigrants," he said. "They're going to end up on the back burner of the global economy."

Here Illegally, Working Hard and Paying Taxes

By Eduardo Porter
June 19, 2006

It is 5:30 in the evening as Adriana makes her way to work against a flow of people streaming out of the lattice of downtown stores and office towers here. She punches a time card, dons a uniform and sets out to clean her first bathroom of the night.

A few miles away, Ana arrives at a suburban Target store at 10 p.m. to clean the in-house restaurant for the next day's shoppers. At 5:30 the next morning,

Emilio starts his rounds at the changing rooms at a suburban department store. A half-hour later, Polo rushes to clean the showers and locker room at a university here before the early birds in the pool finish their morning swim.

Adriana, 27; Ana, 27; Emilio, 48; and Polo, 52, are all illegal immigrants, denizens of one of the most easily overlooked corners of the nation's labor force and almost universally ignored by

the workers, shoppers and students they clean up after.

"It's like you are invisible," Adriana said.

Invisible, perhaps, but not hidden. In contrast to the typical image of an illegal immigrant—paid in cash, working under the table for small-scale labor contractors on a California farm or a suburban construction site—a majority now work for mainstream companies, not fly-by-night operators, and are hired and paid like any other American worker.

Polo—who, like all the workers named in this article, agreed to be interviewed only if his full identity was protected—is employed by a subsidiary of ABM Industries, a publicly traded company based in San Francisco with 73,000 workers across the country and annual revenues of $2.6 billion. Emilio works for the Kimco Corporation, a large private company with 5,000 employees in 30 states and sales of about $100 million.

More than half of the estimated seven million immigrants toiling illegally in the United States get a regular paycheck every week or two, experts say. At the end of the year they receive a W-2 form. Come April 15, many file income tax returns using special ID numbers issued by the Internal Revenue Service

taking over hundreds of small local operators. That activity has gone hand-in-hand with the steady advance of immigrants, legal and illegal—almost all of them Hispanic—who have been drawn into what was once an overwhelmingly American-born work force.

Adriana works for Harvard Maintenance, a New York contractor that has some 3,700 janitors and cleans landmarks like Yankee Stadium and Shea Stadium. ABM Industries, Polo's employer, is the biggest contractor in Minneapolis and St. Paul, with about 35 percent of the market and a portfolio of high-profile customers that include the Minneapolis-Saint Paul International Airport and some downtown buildings.

ABM is a coast-to-coast force in the business, responsible for cleaning a virtual Who's Who of the nation's best-known buildings, at one time even including the World Trade Center in

fraudulent documentation," it said, "we screen all new hires and make sure they provide proper paperwork."

Buying the Documents

A written statement from ABM said that "if an individual were found to have presented falsified work authorization documents to gain employment, their employment would be terminated." Still, in many cities it would be hard to put together a cleaning crew without resorting to an illegal work force.

Adriana used to work for ABM too, she said. But last year Harvard Maintenance, a rival contractor that entered the Minneapolis market two years ago, won the contract to clean her building. Adriana guesses that except for a couple of legal immigrants from Ecuador and a couple of Somalis, the rest of the three dozen or so janitors on her shift are illegal immigrants.

And when the contractor changed, the work force in her building did not. "All the workers," Adriana said, "are the same ones."

Illegal immigrants operate in a kind of parallel employment universe, structured in many ways like the legal job market but with its own rules and procedures.

To begin with, acquiring the necessary documentation to work is a routine transaction these days. In Minneapolis, one only has to mill about for a few minutes in a Kmart parking lot known to immigrants and a young Guatemalan with a Patrón tequila hat will approach on his bike and quietly offer to help.

A set of Polaroid photos can be purchased for $10 at the photo outlet–sporting goods store up the street—a quick snap against a white backdrop tucked among the soccer balls and jerseys of national squads from all over the world.

The documents themselves cost $110. Within two hours of having received the photos, the Guatemalan is cycling back into the parking lot to make the drop of the ID package. It includes a green card with the customer's photo and somebody's fingerprints, along with a Social Security card, for which the number was plucked out of thin air.

More than half of the estimated seven million immigrants toiling illegally in the United States get a regular paycheck every week or two.

so foreigners can pay taxes. Some even get a refund check in the mail.

And they are now present in low-skilled jobs across the country. Illegal immigrants account for 12 percent of workers in food preparation occupations, for instance, according to an analysis of census data by the Pew Hispanic Center. In total, they account for an estimated one in 20 workers in the United States.

The building maintenance industry—a highly competitive business where the company with the lowest labor costs tends to win the contract—has welcomed them with open arms. According to the Pew Hispanic Center, more than a quarter of a million illegal immigrants are janitors, 350,000 are maids and housekeepers and 300,000 are groundskeepers.

The janitorial industry has been transformed in recent years as a handful of companies have consolidated by

New York, where several illegal janitors died on 9/11.

Despite a murky legal status, ABM hired Polo just as it would hire any other worker. His wife and daughter—who already worked at the university—recommended him to their supervisor, who collected Polo's application and paperwork, gave him an ABM uniform and put him on the payroll. He makes $11.75 an hour, has health insurance and gets two weeks of paid vacation every year.

The Immigration Reform and Control Act of 1986 made it a crime for companies to knowingly hire illegal immigrants. Employers say they do their utmost to comply.

"We don't ever knowingly hire undocumented workers," said Amy Polakow, a spokeswoman for Kimco.

Harvard Maintenance issued a statement: "While we are dismayed that an employee allegedly has submitted

Some illegal immigrants do not even need the green card. Until the late 1990's, Mexican illegal immigrants typically arrived in Minnesota with their birth certificate and Mexican voting card, which could be used to obtain a legal Minnesota state ID.

But getting a Social Security number could be a little more complicated in the old days. Lily, 38, another janitor cleaning a building downtown, knew no one in Minneapolis when she arrived illegally from Guatemala 14 years ago. So when a neighbor said she needed papers, she called the smuggler who brought her across the border at his home in Mexico.

He asked her to make up a nine-digit number, which she did by combining the date she left Guatemala and the date she arrived in the United States two months later. She sent him some photos and $75 and received her fake papers by return mail.

Documents in hand, getting a job is straightforward. A common first step for new immigrants is to apply to a temporary work agency for the first job. But as immigrant communities have grown, new arrivals have been able to tap into networks of friends, relatives and former neighbors to help them navigate the United States and jump straight into a permanent job.

When Adriana and her sister arrived in Minneapolis from Mexico in 1998, their mother was waiting for them. She paid the smuggling fee of $1,700 per person and helped Adriana into her first job at the building where she worked and where she knew the supervisor well.

"You know, it's the chain," Adriana said. "I just got a job in my building for a cousin."

In some industries with many illegal immigrants, like construction, farming and landscaping, employers often turn to labor contractors to assemble crews of workers—transferring onto them the responsibility of checking the paperwork. That helps establish deniability in case of an immigration raid.

By contrast, the big building maintenance contractors do much of the hiring themselves. But some still distance themselves from the job market itself by delegating hiring to supervisors in individual buildings—often immigrants themselves—who will receive the job applications, help fill in official documents and copy supporting papers.

Adriana said she never had to step into ABM's offices, which are across the Mississippi River from downtown Minneapolis. She said that the supervisor knew she did not have proper papers.

Cheaper Labor

Starting about 30 years ago, as illegal immigration began to swell, building maintenance contractors in big immigrant hubs like Los Angeles started hiring the new immigrant workers as part of a broader effort to drive down labor costs. Unions for janitors fell apart as landlords shifted to cheaper nonunion contractors to clean their buildings. Wages fell and many American-born workers left the industry.

Between 1970 and 2000, the share of Hispanic immigrants among janitors in Los Angeles jumped from 10 percent to more than 60 percent, according to a forthcoming book by Ruth Milkman, a sociologist at the University of California, Los Angeles, titled "L.A. Story: Work, Immigration and Unionism in America's Second City." (Russell Sage Foundation, August 2006.)

The pattern repeated itself as immigrants spread throughout the rest of the country. By 2000, Hispanic immigrants made up nearly 1 in 5 janitors in the United States, according to Ms. Milkman's research, up from fewer than 1 in 20 in 1980.

When the Service Employees International Union started to reorganize the industry in the late 1990's, it adapted its approach in some cities to appeal to illegal workers. For instance, union contracts in Los Angeles include clauses instructing employers to contact the union if an immigration official "appears on or near the premises" and barring the employers from revealing a worker's name or address to immigration authorities.

Building maintenance contractors and those who contract their services underscore their efforts to keep illegal immigrants off the payroll. But beyond that they are reluctant to discuss the presence of illegal immigrants in the janitorial work force.

In a statement, Target pointed out that its stores were cleaned by outside contractors. "As in the past," it read, "if we find any illegal behavior by our vendor, we will immediately terminate their contract."

Mr. Mitchell said ABM had "put in place policies, procedures and ongoing managerial training for compliance with immigration law." Harvard Maintenance's statement added that "we believe our screening programs currently in place are among the best in the building services industry."

For all these efforts, however, it is remarkably easy for illegal immigrants to get a regular, above-board job.

The law requires employers to make workers fill out I-9 "employment eligibility" forms and provide documents to prove they are legally entitled to work.

But the employers benefit from one large loophole: they are not expected to distinguish between a fake ID and the real thing. To work, illegal immigrants do not need to come up with masterpieces of ID fraud, only something that looks plausible. "To bring a criminal prosecution we need to show an employer knowingly hired an illegal immigrant," said Dean Boyd, a spokesman at Immigration and Customs Enforcement, the branch of the Department of Homeland Security that enforces immigration rules. "'Knowingly' is the key word." Yet the standard of plausibility is not particularly tight. "Some of these documents are so visibly wrong that you don't need to be an expert on what a Social Security card looks like," said Michael Mahdesian, chairman of the board of Servicon Systems, a private contractor that cleans aerospace and defense facilities as well as office buildings in California, Arizona and New Mexico.

Mr. Mahdesian said Servicon was more careful than other contractors—forced by the nature of its clients in the military industry to make more rigorous checks to keep illegal immigrants out. But he said that each time Servicon took over a cleaning contract in a new office building, it found that 25 percent to 30 percent of the workers it inherited from the previous contractor were working illegally, and had to let them go.

"Most companies in this industry doing commercial office buildings take the view that it is not their job to be the immigration service," Mr. Mahdesian said.

Companies have little to fear. The penalty for knowingly hiring illegal immigrants includes up to six months in jail—or up to five years in particularly egregious cases—and fines that range from $275 to $11,000 for each worker. Yet fines are typically negotiated down, and employers are almost always let off the hook. Only 46 people were convicted in 2004 for hiring illegal immigrants; the annual number has been roughly the same for the last decade.

In a rare raid, about 50 illegal workers—including a handful of ABM janitors—were arrested at the Minneapolis-St. Paul airport in 2002, according to Tim Counts, a spokesman for the Minnesota office of immigration and customs enforcement. With one exception—the Wok & Roll Chinese restaurant in the airport terminal—no charges were brought against the companies that hired them, Mr. Counts said.

Pushing for Unionization

Despite becoming a fixture of the labor market, illegal immigrants remain vulnerable at work. Wages declined as illegal immigrants entered the janitorial labor pool. Janitors' median earnings fell by 3 percent in real terms between 1983 and 2002, when the Labor Department changed the definitions of building maintenance jobs and other occupations.

Meanwhile, earnings across all occupations rose by 8 percent, after accounting for inflation. Though unionization has helped push janitors wages back up in many cities, they remain lower in markets with many illegal immigrants in the labor force.

In New York City, janitors cleaning commercial buildings make $19 an hour. Mike Fishman, president of the Service Employees International Union's local in New York, points out that the union never lost ground in the city, and it is still unusual to find illegal immigrants cleaning office buildings there.

In Southern California, by contrast, unions were decimated in the 1980's, and only started recovering in the late 1990's. According to Mike Garcia, president of the union's main local in the state, Southern California's unionized janitors earn between $8.50 and $11 an hour.

Unscrupulous employers still victimize illegal workers frequently. Veronica, a 39-year old illegal immigrant from Mexico, had been working for a temporary employment agency for about a year, crating boxes of beauty products for Aveda, when the agency fired her, then rehired her under a different Social Security number to avoid paying her for the vacation time she had earned.

"They don't want you to gain seniority," she said.

When Adriana started her cleaning job downtown, she said, the supervisor recorded her on the payroll under a different name. But rather than change the entry onABM's payroll, he asked her to buy a set of documents with the new name—forcing her to live for years with two identities, one for work and one for everything else.

Adriana only managed to recover her real name by tagging it on as a middle name when Harvard took over the contract at her building and she re-applied for her job. Now, the name on her state ID is similar to the one on her Social Security card and paycheck.

Many get caught using bad Social Security numbers and lose their jobs. The Social Security Administration sends "no match" letters every year to about eight million workers and about 130,000 employers. Though the letter warns employers not to fire workers because of the mismatch, many do.

Lily, the Guatemalan immigrant, used to clean the offices of General Mills in suburban Minneapolis for a building contractor named Aramark. Earlier this year, she said, the company fired her and other workers, stating that it had received a letter from the government claiming the workers' Social Security numbers were wrong.

"They wanted to get rid of the people the supervisor didn't like," Lily said.

In a statement, Aramark said it "fully complies with federal laws and guidelines regarding employment eligibility, and has procedures in place to confirm employment eligibility of our employees. Should we discover that an employee does not have proper documentation, their employment with Aramark is terminated."

It added that it did not fire workers simply on receipt of a "no match" letter, but gave workers up to 90 days to fix the problem.

The one thing that illegal immigrants did not have to worry about, at least until recently, was the immigration police.

But life has been getting tougher. Minnesota, for instance, tightened its requirements to award state ID's or driver's licenses.

And, lately, immigration authorities have been pursuing illegal immigrants more aggressively. Since April, there have been high-profile raids at several work sites across the country, including IFCO Systems, a pallet and shipping container maker, where agents apprehended nearly 1,200 illegal workers and some managers.

Since Oct. 1, 2005, Immigration and Customs Enforcement has arrested more than 2,100 people in "work site enforcement investigations," compared with 1,145 for the entire previous fiscal year and 845 in fiscal 2004. It is also bringing more serious charges—such as harboring illegal immigrants and money-laundering of illicit profits—against employers who hire them.

Agents have also been sweeping through Minneapolis and other cities, seizing immigrants who had been served with deportation orders and expelling them from the country.

But immigrants adapt. Pablo Tapia, the leader of a church-based community group, has been holding tutorials for immigrants on how to avoid being deported. One rule is "don't open the door" if immigration authorities come knocking. Another is "stay calm and do not run" if agents raid the workplace.

"Just keep working," Mr. Tapia recommends. "If you run, it can be used against you in court."

On Lucille Avenue, the Immigration Debate

By Nina Bernstein
June 26, 2006

The streets where Patrick Nicolosi sees America unraveling still have the look of the 1950's. Single-family homes sit side by side, their lawns weed-whacked into submission to the same suburban dream that Mr. Nicolosi's Italian-American parents embraced 40 years ago when they moved to this working-class community on Long Island.

But when a school bus stops at the white Cape Cod opposite his house, two children seem to pop up from beneath the earth. Emerging from an illegal basement apartment that successive homeowners have rented to a Mexican family of illegal immigrants, they head off to another day of public schooling at taxpayer expense.

This is a neighborhood in the twilight zone of illegal immigration, and wherever Mr. Nicolosi looks, the hidden costs of cheap labor hit home.

There is the gas station a dozen blocks away where more than 100 immigrant day laborers gather, leaving garbage and distress along a residential side street—and undercutting wages for miles, contends Mr. Nicolosi, 49, a third-generation union man and former Wonder Bread truck driver who retired after a back injury. There are the schools and hospitals filled with children from illegal apartments like the basement dwelling, which Mr. Nicolosi calls "a little dungeon, windowless."

"Two children are in school, and one is handicapped—that's $10,000 for elementary school, $100,000 a year for special education," he said. "Why am I paying taxes to support that house?"

One man's frustration over a family in a basement goes a long way toward explaining the grass-roots anger over immigration policy that many members of Congress say they keep hearing in their districts. And it also illustrates the unsettling consequences such anger can set in motion.

It is the economics of class, not the politics of culture or race, that fires Mr. Nicolosi's resentment about what he sees in Elmont, which is probably as diverse a suburb as exists in the United States. Like many working-class Americans who live close to illegal immigrants, he worries that they are yet another force undermining the way of life and the social contract that generations of workers strived so hard to achieve.

"The rich, they're totally oblivious to this situation—what the illegal immigration, the illegal housing, the day labor is doing to us," he said. "Everyone's exploiting these people—the landlords, the contractors. And now we can't afford to pay taxes. People like me who want to live the suburban dream, we're being pushed out unless we join the illegality."

Instead, unlike most people, Mr. Nicolosi joins the civic fray. A self-appointed watchdog, he tries to get local officials to investigate houses that he and his allies suspect of violations, and to crack down on day laborers spilling into front yards.

But this spring, as the immigration debate ignited nationally, the results of his crusade unfolded like a parable about being careful what you wish for—leaving the Mexican family uprooted, neighbors unhappy, and Mr. Nicolosi himself more frustrated than ever.

Elmont, just over the Nassau County line from Queens, has always drawn immigrants or their children. In the decades since Mr. Nicolosi's father, a bus driver, moved his family here from the city, families from every continent have joined the Italian and Central European generations who settled the first subdivisions. Its population of 33,000 is about 46 percent white, 35 percent black and 9 percent Asian, and 14 percent of its residents are Hispanic.

Mr. Nicolosi, a compact, animated man, says he is fighting to save the modest suburban lifestyle that these families seek, regardless of ethnicity.

In the last four years, Elmont raised school taxes by 57 percent and added 40 elementary school classrooms—partly filled, district officials agree, by families in illegal rentals, both immigrant and native-born. In response, Mr. Nicolosi ran for the school board three times, losing yet again in May. As president of the Elmont East End Civic Association, he prods the police to enforce laws against loitering, and in letters to newspapers laments the erosion of suburbia with examples uncomfortably close to home.

Recently, for example, to the dismay of his wife, a police crossing guard, he publicly cited their children—a doctor, a teacher and a law school applicant—as examples of a generation that is being priced out of Long Island by soaring property taxes.

The Cape Cod across Lucille Avenue from Mr. Nicolosi's home is among hundreds of houses that he and his associates have turned in to officials since 2002, he said, based on anonymous complaints collected by a local weekly. They checked the addresses for telltale signs like multiple electric meters—with no regard, he insisted, to the occupants' ethnicity or citizenship.

But even among those who echoed Mr. Nicolosi's concerns, many called him a busybody and a troublemaker. There was sympathy for the family in the basement, and for their landlords, the Cervonis, a young couple with a baby and a construction business who bought the house from an absentee landlord in 2004 and moved in.

"What could we do, throw them out?" asked Luciana Cervoni, who called the tenants hard-working and quiet. "They've lived here for six, seven years now."

In a dungeon?

"If that were the case, we would have moved a long time ago," said the mother in the basement, Ariana O., 30, allowing a glimpse of its two-bedroom finished interior that showed how homey the couple had made it for their three children: a boy of 10, a developmentally disabled girl of about 6, and a year-old baby—the last two born in the United States.

Ms. O. and her husband, Placido, a mason, asked that their last name be withheld, for fear of immigration authorities. They were aware of past housing-code citations generated by Mr. Nicolosi's complaints. Nothing had come of those, so they were not too worried.

But as the national debate flared, so did Mr. Nicolosi's frustration at what he saw in his neighborhood. Those clipped front lawns? Mowed by underpaid Latino workers. Those tidy homes? Contractors hired immigrants off the books to repair roofs and replace pipes, Mr. Nicolosi said, instead of training, and decently compensating, someone like the 20-year-old American up the block who needed a job.

"They're telling us Americans don't want to do these jobs," Mr. Nicolosi said. "That's a lie. The business owners don't want to pay. I know what my grandparents fought for: fair wages and days off. Now we're doing it in reverse."

Trying not to feed the cycle, Mr. Nicolosi said, he had paid a premium to use nationally known home-improvement chains when he renovated his house. But by now he knew that was no guarantee that the people who did the work were legal, let alone fairly paid, he said.

"It's either a country of law and order and what my parents fought for, or we just turn it over to big business," he went on, working himself into a speech that connected many dots.

He pointed to American companies in Mexico that paid wages too low to keep Mexicans from streaming north to sell their labor on American streets. He angrily denied bigotry and avowed pity for the immigrants, squeezed by low wages and high rents.

"They will never, ever better themselves," he said of the Mexican family.

And as he drove his black S.U.V. through a neighborhood where garden shrines outnumber basketball hoops, his world view darkened what he saw. Passing a small house, he shared his suspicion that it illegally harbored multiple immigrant families, because a dozen children regularly played out front.

But the homeowners later set the record straight. "We're a family here—we're no immigrants," declared Fanny Echeverria, 40, quickly adding, "What makes him better than immigrants?"

She and her husband, George, have five children between them, and their yard is a magnet for neighbors' children. Ms. Echeverria is a native New Yorker of Greek and Dominican heritage, her husband a naturalized United States citizen born in Chile. And they own one of Long Island's most highly rated French restaurants, Soigné, in Woodmere.

Indeed, Mr. Echeverria's biography served as a counterpoint to Mr. Nicolosi's pessimism. He was 10 when his family came to America in 1979, and he was an illegal immigrant himself until the 1986 amnesty.

Still, he echoed Mr. Nicolosi's concerns about immigrants in unsafe basement apartments. "They cannot get a steady job because they are here illegally, so they cannot pay for housing," he said.

On the other hand, they avoid middle-class tax burdens, Mr. Nicolosi contends, sounding almost envious. He and a neighbor often joke that they should move to Mexico and return illegally: "Then we don't have to worry about health care, don't have to worry about paying taxes. And if I worked for $100 a day I'd be better off. After I pay taxes I don't even have $100 a day."

From the basement, what struck the Mexican couple, however, was that Mr. Nicolosi did not work.

"The man has nothing to do except look," the wife said in Spanish as her husband cooked dinner. Recalling the Latino workers she saw renovating his house, she added, "If we weren't here, who would do the work?"

"If we weren't here, who would do the work?"

In Guanajuato, Mexico, Mr. O.'s best option was a job at General Motors that at the time paid $10 a day, he said. Like everyone, he added, "we came for a better life for our children."

What of the union battles of Mr. Nicolosi's grandparents? "That's what we're doing now," Ms. O. said. Taxes? "We all consume," Mr. O. argued, with a gesture that took in the dining table, the television and a picture of the Last Supper. "I'm paying the rent, so I'm paying the homeowner's taxes."

But upstairs that day, their landlords were deciding to evict the family. An official had called, alerting them to a new complaint by Mr. Nicolosi, the Cervonis said. This time, with heightened public attention, it would lead to hefty fines unless the basement was vacated.

Joseph Cervoni broke the news to the tenants the night President Bush spoke to the nation about immigration. As word spread, neighbors blamed Mr. Nicolosi. Carolyn Gilbert, a retired secretary who advocates an electrified fence at the Mexican border, said he had no conscience. "People forget the human dimension," she said.

Louise Cerullo, 84, a registered Republican like Mr. Nicolosi, protested: "They're human beings. If they can work and pay their rent, what's wrong with that?"

The talk reached Mr. Nicolosi soon after his school board defeat. He denied complaining, then threatened to sue local officials for identifying him, and questioned the timing of the crackdown.

"They did it now to shut me up," he said.

On the first Saturday in June, the Mexican family moved out. Watching from next door, Ms. Gilbert worried about the children's schooling, and wondered where they could go. Probably, she said, to another basement apartment.

"For every problem, there's a solution," she added. "For every solution there's another problem."

VI. PERSPECTIVES ON RELIGION AND POLITICS

Religion has always been closely associated with politics on the national level, but not quite as significantly as the recent association of conservative Christians and the Republican Party. The first article places this relationship in historical context while the second describes how political agendas can become subject to religious influence. Despite the widespread belief that religious conservatism is virtually synonymous with dissolution of the welfare state and support of the Republican Party, the American public seems to be developing a different perspective. The third article reports some of the recent indicators of change that were so clearly demonstrated in the midterm election results reported in the last article. Is the religious influence on American politics beneficial or detrimental?

As you read the following articles, consider how you would answer these questions.

22. Economic Scene: Red States, Blue States
New Labels for Long-Running Differences (05/04/06)

- Is the nation more polarized today than ever before?
- What has been the "genius of Republicans" since Ronald Reagan was President?

23. Conservative Christians Warn Republicans against Inaction (05/15/06)

- Why is James Dobson accusing the Republican leadership of "betraying the social conservatives?"
- Why is James Dobson's support so important to the Republicans for the 2006 midterm elections?

24. In Poll, Republican Party Slips as a Friend of Religion (08/25/06)

What was the most "startling change" in viewpoint reported in this poll?
How is this change explained?

25. The 2006 Elections: The Voters
Religious Voting Data Show Some Shift, Observers Say (11/09/06)

- What is the "God Gap?"
- What portion of the religious community voted Democrat?

Economic Scene: Red States, Blue States
New Labels for Long-Running Differences

By Hal R. Varian
May 4, 2006

The red state-blue state division has captured the pundits' imaginations, leading to much armchair theorizing about how political constituencies in the United States are evolving.

According to some, the country is splitting into two opposing camps, with political divisions becoming more polarized and more spatially segregated than they have been in the past.

A recent working paper, "Myths and Realities of American Political Geography," by two Harvard University economists, Edward L. Glaeser and Bryce A. Ward, challenges this conventional wisdom. The paper can be downloaded from http://papers.ssrn.com/sol3/papers.cfm?abstract--id=874977.

The economists examined a number of contemporary and historical data sources on cultural, religious, economic and political attitudes and compared these responses across states.

They found that differences in political attitudes across states are nothing new: the Civil War and Roaring Twenties had much larger geographic variation in political views than we do today. Though dispersion in political attitudes has generally declined over the last 60 years, the last four years have brought a small uptick.

Though views have become somewhat less associated with geography in the 20th century, they still show strong differences. The fraction of the voters in a given area who vote Republican correlates well with the fraction who voted Republican in the last election.

Furthermore, America is not becoming more polarized. Of course, Republicans have a more positive view of the Republican Party than the Democratic Party, and vice versa, but attitudes have hardly changed since 1978. It is fair to point out, though, that attitudes seem to have become somewhat more partisan in the last few years.

The most remarkable phenomenon is the rise of religion in politics. Thirty years ago, income was a better prediction of party affiliation than church attendance, but this is no longer true. Religion also played a big role in politics a century ago, so we may well be returning to the historical norm.

Cultural and religious attitudes play a big role in voting behavior. For example, the fraction of the population who agreed with the statement "AIDS is God's punishment for immoral sexual behavior" was highly correlated with whether the state was red or blue, according to surveys conducted by the Pew Research Center. The differences in religious attitudes between Vermont and Mississippi are huge.

These cultural divisions have been around for a long time. In the 1936–37

Another peculiar connection is the strong correlation between religiosity and militarism. Respondents to Pew's survey who agree that "prayer is an important part of my daily life" also agree that the "best way to ensure peace is through military strength."

So why are these cultural and political divisions so persistent? The authors offer both some simple correlations and some more elaborate theories. It turns out that the degree of industrialization 85 years ago is an "astonishingly good predictor of Democratic support" among today's voters, as is the fraction of the population that is foreign-born.

But the biggest effect seems to be the correlation between religion and Republicanism. Among white voters who attend religious services at least once a week, 71 percent voted Republican in the last election, according to the Pew survey.

Thirty years ago, income was a better prediction of party affiliation than church attendance, but this is no longer true.

Gallup poll, residents of New England and the Middle Atlantic states were far more likely than citizens elsewhere to support federally financed health measures aimed at venereal disease, to support a free press and to be willing to vote for Catholic or Jewish candidates.

Consumption patterns seem to be correlated with cultural attitudes. For example, the states with the largest level of wine consumption per capita also tend to have the most liberal political and social attitudes. In vino veritas?

Republicans have traditionally appealed to those with higher incomes. The genius of Republicans, beginning with Ronald Reagan and continuing with Karl Rove, was to bring the religious vote into their party, forming a winning coalition of Main Street businessmen, the very wealthy and evangelical Christians. Strange bedfellows, to be sure, but they win elections.

Mr. Glaeser and Mr. Ward offer some speculation about why religion is such an attractive theme for politicians. According to their theory, direct appeals to voters on issues like abortion are tricky, because strong positions inspire groups on both sides of the issue, who then cancel each other out in votes. The trick is to send "coded messages" to different groups of voters. Strong opponents of abortion, for example, may react positively to certain religious allusions that appear innocuous to mainstream voters.

The Economist magazine characterizes American politics as a contest between the incompetence of Republicans and the incoherence of the Democrats. But there is a reason for the Democrats' incoherence: they are feverishly trying to assemble their own collection of strange bedfellows, and no one quite knows what it is.

Ultimately, both parties face the same challenge: how to keep the support of their cultural and political extremists without giving them so much power that they alienate the middle-of-the-road voters.

In this sort of game, the incumbents tend to have an advantage, unless they are perceived as having messed up so badly that even their most fervent supporters desert them. Hey, maybe the Democrats have a chance after all.

■ Hal R. Varian is a professor of business, economics and information management at the University of California, Berkeley.

Conservative Christians Warn Republicans against Inaction

By David D. Kirkpatrick
May 15, 2006

Some of President Bush's most influential conservative Christian allies are becoming openly critical of the White House and Republicans in Congress, warning that they will withhold their support in the midterm elections unless Congress does more to oppose same-sex marriage, obscenity and abortion.

"There is a growing feeling among conservatives that the only way to cure the problem is for Republicans to lose the Congressional elections this fall," said Richard Viguerie, a conservative direct-mail pioneer.

Mr. Viguerie also cited dissatisfaction with government spending, the war in Iraq and the immigration-policy debate, which Mr. Bush is scheduled to address in a televised speech on Monday night.

"I can't tell you how much anger there is at the Republican leadership," Mr. Viguerie said. "I have never seen anything like it."

In the last several weeks, Dr. James C. Dobson, founder of Focus on the Family and one of the most influential Christian conservatives, has publicly accused Republican leaders of betraying the social conservatives who helped elect them in 2004. He has also warned in private meetings with about a dozen of the top Republicans in Washington that he may turn critic this fall unless the party delivers on conservative goals.

And at a meeting in Northern Virginia this weekend of the Council for National Policy, an alliance of the most prominent Christian conservatives, several participants said sentiment toward the White House and Republicans in Congress had deteriorated sharply since the 2004 elections.

When the group met in the summer of 2004, it resembled a pep rally for Mr. Bush and his allies on Capitol Hill, and one session focused on how to use state initiatives seeking to ban same-sex marriage to help turn out the vote. This year, some participants are complaining that as soon as Mr. Bush was re-elected he stopped expressing his support for a constitutional amendment banning such unions.

Christian conservative leaders have often threatened in the months before an election to withhold their support for Republicans in an effort to press for their legislative goals. In the 1990's, Dr. Dobson in particular became known for his jeremiads against the Republican party, most notably in the months before the 1998 midterm elections.

But the complaints this year are especially significant because they underscore how the broad decline in public approval for Mr. Bush and Congressional Republicans is beginning to cut into their core supporters. The threatened defections come just two years after many Christian conservatives—most notably Dr. Dobson—abandoned much of their previous reservations and poured energy into electing Republicans in 2004.

Dr. Dobson gave his first presidential endorsement to Mr. Bush and held get-out-the-vote rallies that attracted thousands of admirers in states with pivotal Senate races while Focus on the Family and many of its allies helped register voters in conservative churches.

Republican officials, who were granted anonymity to speak publicly because of the sensitivity of the situation, acknowledged the difficult political climate but said they planned to rally conservatives by underscoring the contrast with Democrats and emphasizing the recent confirmations of two conservatives to the Supreme Court.

Midterm Congressional elections tend to be won by whichever side can motivate more true believers to vote. Dr. Dobson and other conservatives are renewing their complaints about the Republicans at a time when several recent polls have shown sharp declines in approval among Republicans and conservatives. And compared with other

Dr. Dobson has made the same point more politely in a series of private conversations over the last two weeks in meetings with several top Republicans, including Karl Rove, the president's top political adviser; Senator Bill Frist of Tennessee, the Republican leader;

Samuel A. Alito Jr. to the Supreme Court, party strategists say the White House and Senate Republicans are escalating their fights against the Democrats over conservative nominees to lower federal courts, and the Senate is set to revive the same-sex marriage debate next month with a vote on the proposed amendment.

But it is unclear how much Congressional Republicans will be able to do for social conservatives before the next election.

"There's just very, very little to show for what has happened, and I think there's going to be some trouble down the road if they don't get on the ball."

constituencies, evangelical Protestants have historically been suspicious of the worldly business of politics and thus more prone to stay home unless they feel clear moral issues are at stake.

"When a president is in a reasonably strong position, these kind of leaders don't have a lot of leverage," said Charlie Cook, a nonpartisan political analyst. "But when the president is weak, they tend to have a lot of leverage."

Dr. Dobson, whose daily radio broadcast has millions of listeners, has already signaled his willingness to criticize Republican leaders. In a recent interview with Fox News on the eve of a visit to the White House, he accused Republicans of "just ignoring those that put them in office."

Dr. Dobson cited the House's actions on two measures that passed over the objections of social conservatives: a hate-crime bill that extended protections to gay people, and increased support for embryonic stem cell research.

"There's just very, very little to show for what has happened," Dr. Dobson said, "and I think there's going to be some trouble down the road if they don't get on the ball."

According to people who were at the meetings or were briefed on them,

Representative J. Dennis Hastert of Illinois, the House speaker; and Representative John A. Boehner of Ohio, the majority leader.

"People are getting concerned that they have not seen some of these issues move forward that were central to the 2004 election," said Tony Perkins, president of the Family Research Council, who attended the meetings.

Richard D. Land, a top official of the Southern Baptist Convention who has been one of Mr. Bush's most loyal allies, said in an interview last week that many conservatives were upset that Mr. Bush had not talked more about a constitutional amendment to ban same-sex marriage.

"A lot of people are disappointed that he hasn't put as much effort into the marriage amendment as he did for the prescription drug benefit or Social Security reform," Dr. Land said.

Republicans say they are taking steps to revive their support among Christian conservatives. On Thursday night, Mr. Rove made the case for the party at a private meeting of the Council for National Policy, participants said.

In addition to reminding conservatives of the confirmations of Chief Justice John G. Roberts Jr. and Justice

No one expects the same-sex marriage amendment to pass this year. Republican leaders have not scheduled votes on a measure to outlaw transporting minors across state lines for abortions, and the proposal faces long odds in the Senate. A measure to increase obscenity fines for broadcasters is opposed by media industry trade groups, pitting Christian conservatives against the business wing of the party, and Congressional leaders have not committed to bring it to a vote.

Grover Norquist, president of Americans for Tax Reform and another frequent participant in the Council for National Policy, argued that Christian conservatives were hurting their own cause.

"If the Republicans do poorly in 2006," Mr. Norquist said, "the establishment will explain that it was because Bush was too conservative, specifically on social and cultural issues."

Dr. Dobson declined to comment. His spokesman, Paul Hetrick, said that Dr. Dobson was "on a fact-finding trip to see where Republicans are regarding the issues that concern values voters most, especially the Marriage Protection Act," and that it was too soon to tell the results.

In Poll, Republican Party Slips as a Friend of Religion

By Laurie Goodstein
August 25, 2006

A new poll shows that fewer Americans view the Republican Party as "friendly to religion" than a year ago, with the decline particularly steep among Catholics and white evangelical Protestants—constituencies at the core of the Republicans' conservative Christian voting bloc.

The survey found that the proportion of Americans who say the Republican Party is friendly to religion fell 8 percentage points in the last year, to 47 percent from 55 percent. Among Catholics and white evangelical Protestants, the decline was 14 percentage points.

The Democratic Party suffers from the perception of an even more drastic religion deficit, but that is not new. Just 26 percent of poll respondents said the Democratic Party was friendly to religion, down from 29 percent last year.

The telephone poll, conducted by the Pew Forum on Religion and Public Life and the Pew Research Center for the People and the Press, was conducted July 6–19 among 2,003 adults. The margin of sampling error was

of the Republican Party by its core constituency.

"It's unclear how directly this will translate into voting behavior," Mr. Green said, "but this is a baseline indicator that religious conservatives see the party they've chosen to support as less friendly to religion than they used to."

He speculated that religious conservatives could feel betrayed that some Republican politicians recently voted to back stem cell research, and that a Republican-dominated Congress failed to pass an amendment outlawing same-sex marriage.

"At the minimum, there will be less good will toward the Republican Party by these conservative religious groups, and a disenchantment that the party will be able to deliver on its promises," Mr. Green said.

Americans remained critical of the influence of both the right and the left on religion. Sixty-nine percent agreed that liberals had "gone too far in trying to keep religion out of schools and government"—an increase of three percentage points, which is not statistically

The respondents were almost evenly divided on whether the influence of religion on governmental institutions like the presidency, Congress and the Supreme Court was increasing (42 percent) or decreasing (45 percent). Most of those who said the influence was decreasing said that was "a bad thing."

Americans also disagree on whether churches and houses of worship should express their views on politics, with 51 percent saying they should, and 46 percent saying they should keep out of political matters. This divide has held steady for the last five years, the Pew report said.

Of the topics addressed by clergy members during religious services, 92 percent of respondents who attend religious services regularly said they had heard clergy members speak about hunger and poverty, 59 percent said abortion, 53 percent said Iraq, 52 percent said homosexuality and 40 percent said evolution or intelligent design. Only 24 percent said they heard clergy members discuss stem cell research, and 21 percent immigration.

In the last year, religious organizations, including some representing evangelicals, have made global warming a priority.

In the poll, a large majority (79 percent) said there was "solid evidence" of global warming, and 61 percent said it was a problem that required "immediate government action." But white evangelicals and mainline Protestants were more skeptical about global warming than Catholics and secular Americans were, and more likely to say that it is the result of natural causes, not human activity.

> ## "Religious conservatives see the party they've chosen to support as less friendly to religion than they used to."

plus or minus three to four percentage points, depending on the question.

The survey examined Americans' attitudes on such topics as politics, science, the Bible, global warming and Israel. But the most startling change, said John Green, senior fellow in religion and American politics at the Pew Forum, was the perception

significant. And 49 percent agreed that conservative Christians had "gone too far in trying to impose their religious values on the country," also a three percentage point increase.

Asked about "the Christian conservative movement," 44 percent had a favorable view and 36 percent unfavorable, about the same as a year ago.

The 2006 Elections: The Voters
Religious Voting Data Show Some Shift, Observers Say

By Laurie Goodstein
November 9, 2006
(Correction Appended)

Ever since George W. Bush won a second term two years ago by relying on the turnout of his religious conservative base, Democrats have been intent on siphoning off religious voters.

Some liberal religious advocates proclaimed yesterday that the Democratic sweep showed that their party had succeeded in closing what they called the God Gap. But the results are more mixed than that, according to experts who analyze trends among religious voters.

Defying predictions of widespread disillusionment, white evangelical and born-again Christians did not desert Republican Congressional candidates and they did not stay home, nationwide exit polls show.

When it came to turnout, white evangelicals and born-again Christians made up about 24 percent of those who voted, compared with 23 percent in the 2004 election. And 70 percent of those white evangelical and born-again Christians voted for Republican Congressional candidates nationally, also little changed from the 72 percent who voted for such candidates in 2004.

But in some states, like Ohio and Pennsylvania, Democratic Senate candidates who intentionally tried to appeal to religious voters did succeed at winning back a significant percentage of Roman Catholics and white mainline Protestants.

Ted Strickland, the newly elected governor of Ohio, is a Methodist minister who spoke openly about his faith, and Bob Casey, the victor in Pennsylvania's Senate race, is a Catholic opposed to abortion. They also won over some less religiously active voters, those who attend church once a month or less.

"It looks like the white evangelical base of the Republican Party pretty much held firm," said John Green, a senior fellow with the Pew Forum on Religion and Public Life, said. "The white evangelicals did show up, and they did vote Republican."

"The biggest change appears to be in the states where the Democratic candidates made a real effort to attract these religious voters," Mr. Green said. "It seems to have paid off."

Never before in any election had the religious left been so organized and so active. They held rallies and passed out hundreds of thousands of voter guides, all with the message that religious conservatives' traditional agenda of opposition to abortion and same-sex marriage was too narrow. With the help of religious liberals, six states passed ballot initiatives calling for a raise in the minimum wage.

"This was a significant shift in the religious vote, where you see a reclaiming of the values debate," said Alexia Kelley, executive director of Catholics in Alliance for the Common Good, a liberal group formed after the last election to counter Catholic conservatives.

In Ohio, voters elected all four state board of education candidates who opposed the teaching of intelligent design, and victories like that gave religious liberals cause to proclaim the end of the right's dominance of religious voters.

Bobby Clark, deputy director of ProgressNow, a liberal group in Colorado, said, "After 2004, people were saying that the religious right owns this country now. Far from it. They have networks and the ability to move quickly and to dominate the airwaves, but they do not represent most Americans. Most Americans are pretty moderate people."

In Colorado and seven other states, voters approved constitutional amendments defining marriage as a union between a man and a woman. Arizona was the only state in which such an amendment was defeated.

Yet religious conservatives were reeling yesterday. The Rev. Troy Newman, president of the anti-abortion Operation Rescue, called Election Day Bloody Tuesday because of a string of defeats. Among them were a sweeping initiative in South Dakota that would have outlawed most abortions; a proposition in California that would have required parents to be notified when minors have abortions; and the attorney general in Kansas, Phill Kline, who has investigated abortion clinics.

Mr. Newman said that many religious leaders he knew had remained silent or had endorsed Democrats. "The pulpits of America bear responsibility," he said. "I believe God will hold them accountable for that."

> *Never before in any election had the religious left been so organized and so active.*

The shifts in the Catholic vote were the most noteworthy. In Ohio, according to exit polls, Democrats picked up 20 percent more of that constituency than they had in 2000; in Pennsylvania, they picked up 11 percent more. The comparison is not exact, however, because 2000 involved a presidential election, not a midterm election. Data for the 2002 midterm election in those states are not available.

(Comparisons of evangelical voters are unreliable because exit poll questions designed to identify evangelicals changed from one election to another.)

The religious voters who did switch from Republican to Democrat just mirrored the American electorate as a whole, said James L. Guth, a professor of political science and adviser for the College Republicans at Furman University in Greenville, S.C.

■ **Correction:** November 11, 2006, Saturday. An article on Thursday about election turnout by religious voters misstated the number of states where constitutional amendments defining marriage as a union between a man and a woman were approved Tuesday. It is seven, not eight.

VII. PERSPECTIVES ON DISCRIMINATION AND CIVIL RIGHTS

While it may be easy to think of the battle for civil rights and an end to discrimination as a distant historical struggle, the articles selected in this section demonstrate that the battle continues even today. The first article compares the human rights struggle of undocumented immigrants with the civil rights struggle of African-Americans. Post–September 11 events suggest, in the second article, that new shades of discrimination remain possible. In this case, the insecurity of Arab-Americans has increased as law enforcement has concentrated more attention on this segment of our society. The third article celebrates a recent U.S. Supreme Court decision that strengthens the civil rights protection of every employee in the country, and the fourth suggests that the elimination of inequities is not always as easy as one may presume.

As you read the following articles, consider how you would answer these questions.

26. Growing Unease for Some Blacks on Immigration (05/04/06)

- Why are some African American leaders "uneasy" with illegal immigrants describing their political fight as a "new civil rights movement?"
- In what way is the immigrant struggle similar to the African American struggle for human rights?

27. After 9/11, Arab-Americans Fear Police Acts, Study Finds (06/12/06)

- What is the religion of most Arab-Americans?
- Why are Arab-Americans now distrustful of law enforcement officials?

28. Supreme Court Gives Employees Broader Protection against Retaliation in Workplace (06/23/06)

- What is the new definition for retaliation?
- How does employee protection from employer retaliation differ from employee protection from discrimination?

29. Meaning of "Normal" Is at Heart of Gay Marriage Ruling (07/08/06)

- Did the New York Court of Appeals conclude that gays and lesbians are discriminated against because they cannot marry?
- Did the New York Court of Appeals support gay and lesbian marriage?

Growing Unease for Some Blacks on Immigration

By Rachel L. Swarns
May 4, 2006

In their demonstrations across the country, some Hispanic immigrants have compared the Rev. Dr. Martin Luther King Jr.'s struggle to their own, singing "We Shall Overcome" and declaring a new civil rights movement to win citizenship for millions of illegal immigrants.

Civil rights stalwarts like the Rev. Jesse Jackson; Representative John Lewis, Democrat of Georgia; Julian Bond and the Rev. Joseph E. Lowery have hailed the recent protests as the natural progression of their movement in the 1960's.

But despite some sympathy for the nation's illegal immigrants, many black professionals, academics and blue-collar workers feel increasingly uneasy as they watch Hispanics flex their political muscle while assuming the mantle of a seminal black struggle for justice.

Some blacks bristle at the comparison between the civil rights movement and the immigrant demonstrations, pointing out that black protesters in the 1960's were American citizens and had endured centuries of enslavement, rapes, lynchings and discrimination before they started marching.

Others worry about the plight of low-skilled black workers, who sometimes compete with immigrants for entry-level jobs.

And some fear the unfinished business of the civil rights movement will fall to the wayside as America turns its attention to a newly energized Hispanic minority with growing political and economic clout.

"All of this has made me start thinking, 'What's going to happen to African-Americans?'" said Brendon L. Laster, 32, a black fund-raiser at Howard University here, who has been watching the marches. "What's going to happen to our unfinished agenda?"

Mr. Laster is dapper and cosmopolitan, a part-time professor and Democratic activist who drinks and dines with a wide circle of black, white and Hispanic friends. He said he marveled at first as the images of cheering, flag-waving immigrants flickered across his television screen. But as some demonstrators proclaimed a new civil rights movement, he grew uncomfortable.

He says that immigrant protesters who claim the legacy of Dr. King and Rosa Parks are going too far. And he has begun to worry about the impact that the emerging immigrant activism will have on black Americans, many of whom still face poverty, high rates of unemployment and discrimination in the workplace.

"I think what they were able to do, the level of organization they were able to pull off, that was phenomenal," said Mr. Laster, who is also a part-time sociology professor at a community college in Baltimore. "But I do think their struggle is, in fundamental ways, very different from ours. We didn't chose to come here; we came here as slaves. And we were denied, even though we were legal citizens, our basic rights."

"There are a still lot of unresolved issues from the civil rights era," he said. "Perhaps we're going to be pushed to the back burner."

This painful debate is bubbling up in church halls and classrooms, on call-in radio programs and across dining room tables. Some blacks prefer to discuss the issue privately for fear of alienating their Hispanic allies. But others are publicly airing their misgivings, saying they are too worried to stay silent.

"We will have no power, no clout," warned Linda Carter-Lewis, 62, a human resources manager and the branch president of the N.A.A.C.P. in Des Moines. "That's where I see this immigrant movement going. Even though so many thousands and thousands of them have no legal status and no right to vote right now, that day is coming."

Immigrant leaders defend their use of civil rights language, saying strong parallels exist between the two struggles. And they argue that their movement will ultimately become a powerful vehicle to fight for the rights of all American workers, regardless of national origin.

"African-Americans during the civil rights movement were in search of the American dream and that's what our movement is trying to achieve for our community," said Jaime Contreras, president of the National Capital Immigration Coalition, which organized the April 10 demonstration that drew tens of thousands of people to Washington.

"We face the same issues even if we speak different languages."

"We face the same issues even if we speak different languages," said Mr. Contreras, who is from El Salvador and listens to Dr. King's speeches for inspiration.

Mr. Jackson, who addressed the immigrant rally on Monday in New York, echoed those views. He noted that Dr. King, at the end of his life, focused on improving economic conditions for all Americans, regardless of race. And he said the similarities between African-Americans and illegal immigrants were too powerful to ignore.

"We too were denied citizenship," Mr. Jackson said. "We too were un-documented workers working without wages, without benefits, without the vote. "We should feel honored that other people are using tactics and strategies from our struggle. We shouldn't say they're stealing from us. They're learning from us."

Mr. Jackson said corporate employers were fueling the tensions between blacks and immigrants by refusing to pay a living wage to all workers. John Campbell, a black steel worker and labor activist from Iowa, agreed.

"This is a class issue," said Mr. Campbell, who has been disheartened by black critics of the immigrant marches. "We need to join forces. We can't improve our lot in life as African-Americans by suppressing the rights of anyone else."

But blacks and immigrants have long had a history of uneasy relations in the United States.

W. E. B. DuBois, a founder of the N.A.A.C.P., and other prominent black leaders worried that immigrants would displace blacks in the work-place. Ronald Walters, director of the African-American Leadership Institute at the University of Maryland, said blacks cheered when the government restricted Asian immigration to the United States after World War I. And many Europeans who came to this country discriminated against blacks.

Blacks and Hispanics have also been allies. In the 1960's, Dr. King and Cesar Chavez, the Mexican-American farm labor leader, corresponded with each other. And when Mr. Chavez was jailed, Dr. King's widow, Coretta Scott King, visited him in jail, Mr. Walters said. In recent years, blacks and Hispanics have been influential partners in the Democratic Party.

A recent poll conducted by the Pew Hispanic Center captured the ambivalence among blacks over immigration. Nearly 80 percent said immigrants from Latin American work very hard and have strong family values.

But nearly twice as many blacks as whites said that they or a family member had lost a job, or not gotten a job, because an employer hired an immigrant worker. Blacks were also more likely than whites to feel that immigrants take jobs away from American citizens.

Mr. Walters said he understood those conflicting emotions, saying he feels torn himself because of his concerns about the competition between immigrants and low-skilled black men for jobs. In 2004, 72 percent of black male high school dropouts in their 20's were jobless, compared with 34 percent of white and 19 percent of Hispanic dropouts.

"I applaud them moving out of the shadows and into the light because of the human rights issues involved," Mr. Walters said of illegal immigrants. "I've given my entire life to issues of social justice as an activist and an academic. In that sense, I'm with them.

"But they also represent a powerful ingredient to the perpetuation of our struggle," he said. "We have a problem where half of black males are unemployed in several cities. I can't ignore that and simply be my old progressive self and say it's not an issue. It is an issue."

After 9/11, Arab-Americans Fear Police Acts, Study Finds

By Andrea Elliott
June 12, 2006

In the aftermath of Sept. 11, Arab-Americans have a greater fear of racial profiling and immigration enforcement than of falling victim to hate crimes, according to a national study financed by the Justice Department.

The study also concluded that local police officers and federal agents were straining under the pressure to fight terrorism, and that new federal policies in this effort were poorly defined and inconsistently applied.

The two-year study, released today by the Vera Institute of Justice, explored the changed relationship between Arab-Americans and law enforcement in the years since the 2001 terrorist attacks. The Vera Institute is a nonprofit policy research center based in New York.

About 100 Arab-Americans and 111 law enforcement personnel, both F.B.I. agents and police officers, participated in the study, which was conducted from 2003 to 2005. Some respondents were interviewed privately and others took part in focus groups in cities around the nation, which were not identified in order to protect the identities of the respondents.

Both Arab-American community leaders and law enforcement officials interviewed in the study said that cooperation between both groups had suffered from a lack of trust.

"It underscores the importance of community policing, of engaging the Arab and Muslim community in a constructive way and bringing them in to be partners," said Farhana Khera, the executive director of Muslim Advocates, a national nonprofit organization of lawyers.

While Muslims represent a spectrum of ethnic and national backgrounds, the study focused on Arab-Americans in order to understand the experience of one group more deeply, said Nicole Henderson, the lead author of the report. An estimated two-thirds of Arab-Americans are Christian.

Arab-Americans reported an increasing sense of victimization, suspicion of government and law enforcement, and concerns about protecting their civil liberties, according to the study, which was paid for by the National Institute of Justice, a research agency of the Justice Department.

A fear of surveillance ranked high among their concerns. During one focus group, a woman told the story of an encyclopedia salesman who came to her door and asked to use the bathroom. She worried that he might have been an agent trying to plant a listening device in her home.

While hate crimes against Arab-Americans spiked after Sept. 11, they have decreased in the years since, according to both law enforcement and Arab-American respondents.

A series of post-9/11 policies have sown the deepest fear among Arab-Americans, including unease about the USA Patriot Act, voluntary interviews of thousands of Arab-Americans by federal agents, and an initiative known as Special Registration, in which more than 80,000 immigrant men were fingerprinted, photographed and questioned by authorities.

These new measures threatened to harm decades of work by police departments to build trust in their communities, especially among immigrants, the study concluded. After 9/11, federal agents increasingly turned to the police for help with gathering intelligence and enforcing immigration laws, Ms. Henderson said.

F.B.I. agents were also given expanded powers to arrest people for immigration violations in connection with terrorism cases.

The study concluded that there was confusion among both F.B.I. agents and the local police about their roles in enforcing immigration, and that their resources had been stretched thin by counterterrorism initiatives.

John Miller, an assistant director for the Federal Bureau of Investigation, said the report confirmed many of the realities facing the bureau.

"We have finite resources and tremendous responsibilities," Mr. Miller said. "When you take 40 percent of your resources and turn them towards national security issues in the wake of Sept. 11 because of a significant and

Arab-Americans reported an increasing sense of victimization, suspicion of government and law enforcement, and concerns about protecting their civil liberties.

demonstrable threat, you're going to see a strain on resources."

The degree to which police officers have enforced immigration laws varied, according to the study: Some departments formally deputized officers to arrest people for immigration violations, while other departments left this to the discretion of officers.

Both Arab-Americans and law enforcement personnel expressed dismay about the reporting of false information in the form of anonymous tips. F.B.I. agents said they had responded to calls stemming from petty disputes, business competition and dating rivalries, according to the study.

"It reminds me of Syria," an Arab-American was quoted as saying in the study. "If someone wants to get you, they will call the police."

Both Arab-Americans and law enforcement respondents acknowledged that the relationship between them was necessary, but could be improved.

Mr. Miller said the process would take time.

"We didn't bring this on the community—the terrorists did," he said. "The community is paying for that. We are paying for that as law enforcement because when we're doing our investigations, it seems like we're singling out a group or a religion and the fact is, we're not. We have to go where the leads take us."

In the weeks after Sept. 11, community outreach by the Los Angeles County Sheriff's Department helped engender trust among Muslims, said Sheriff Lee Baca. The department received reports that Pakistani immigrants working at 7-Eleven stores had been harassed. In response, officers visited more than 100 stores in Los Angeles and Orange Counties, he said.

"Our premise here in Los Angeles is that unless we enlist Muslim-American partnerships in the homeland security mission, we are leaving out our greatest resource for preventing terrorist attacks," Sheriff Baca said.

The Vera Institute study concluded that Arab-Americans tended to have a closer relationship with the local police than with federal agents.

James Zogby, president of the Arab American Institute in Washington, said increased surveillance by the F.B.I. had damaged the image many Arab-Americans had of the bureau.

"I think there's more of an arm's length attitude," Mr. Zogby said. "The community still wants very much to cooperate because we know it is important and good to do so, but the cooperation is a one-way street.

"It's, 'Tell us everything you know,' which in most cases is nothing," he said. "What we want is more of a relationship, a partnership, and not to be viewed as just sources."

Supreme Court Gives Employees Broader Protection against Retaliation in Workplace

By Linda Greenhouse
June 23, 2006

The Supreme Court substantially enhanced legal protection against retaliation for employees who complain about discrimination or harassment on the job, in a ruling on Thursday.

The 9-to-0 decision adopted a broadly worded and employee-friendly definition of the type of retaliation that is prohibited by the basic federal law against discrimination in employment.

That law, Title VII of the Civil Rights Act of 1964, prohibits discrimination and prohibits employers from re-taliating against workers who complain about discrimination. But the statute does not define retaliation, leading to disarray among the federal appeals courts and uncertainty for employers and employees alike. Under the standard applied by many courts, it has been almost impossible to win a retaliation case unless the retaliation resulted in dismissal.

By contrast, under the standard the justices adopted on Thursday in an opinion by Justice Stephen G. Breyer, any "materially adverse" employment action that "might have dissuaded a reasonable worker" from complaining about discrimination will count as prohibited retaliation. Depending on the context, retaliation might be found in an unfavorable annual evaluation, an unwelcome schedule change, or other action well short of losing a job.

Retaliation claims make up an important and rapidly growing part of employment law. Some 20,000 retaliation cases were filed with the Equal Employment Opportunity Commission in 2004, a number that has doubled since 1992. The cases now account for more than one-quarter of the federal agency's docket.

"This is an exceptionally important decision that changes the law in most of the country," Eric Schnapper, a law professor at the University of Washington who helped represent the plaintiff in the case, said in an interview.

Lawyers representing employers agreed about the decision's significance,

"This is an exceptionally important decision that changes the law in most of the country."

but with considerably less enthusiasm. Karen Harned, executive director of the National Federation of Independent Business Legal Foundation, said the ruling would lead to "burdensome" litigation and was "particularly disappointing to small employers."

Daniel P. Westman, an employment lawyer with the firm Morrison & Foerster who advises management, said he expected a "huge effect" from the ruling. Mr. Westman said employers would have to take special care to make sure that an employee who lodges a discrimination complaint does not suffer adverse consequences.

The decision upheld a finding of retaliation by a railroad company against a female maintenance worker who was transferred to less desirable duties within her job category and placed on an unpaid leave for 37 days after she complained about sexual harassment. She was reinstated with back pay after a grievance by her union.

A jury awarded $43,500 to the woman, Sheila White, and the United States Court of Appeals for the Sixth Circuit, in Cincinnati, upheld the judgment. The employer, Burlington Northern & Santa Fe Railway Company, appealed to the Supreme Court, arguing that Ms. White had not suffered the type of "tangible employment action" that met the definition of retaliation.

The Bush administration, rejecting the broader standard used by the Equal Employment Opportunity Commission, argued on behalf of the railroad that only those actions that affect an employee's "compensation, terms, conditions, or privileges of employment" should count as retaliation.

Writing for the court on Thursday, Justice Breyer said this argument reflected a misreading of the two relevant sections of Title VII, the one that defines discrimination and the one that prohibits retaliation. The wording of the two is not the same.

While Title VII bars discrimination on the basis of race, sex and religion in the "terms" and "conditions" of employment, "no such limiting words appear in the anti-retaliation provision," Justice Breyer said. He said there was "strong reason to believe" that Congress intended the protection against retaliation to be broader than the protection against discrimination because it wanted to "deter the many forms that effective retaliation can take," in the workplace and beyond.

Consequently, Justice Breyer said, "the anti-retaliation provision, unlike the substantive provision, is not limited to discriminatory actions that affect the terms and conditions of employment."

While agreeing with the other eight justices to uphold the judgment for Ms. White, Justice Samuel A. Alito

Jr. disagreed with the standard, which he said was "unclear" and could lead to "topsy-turvy results." He said the retaliation definition should be limited to "only those discriminatory practices" that Title VII forbids. Ms. White suffered from "adverse" and "tangible" employment actions that met that test, he said.

In the majority opinion, Burlington Northern & Santa Fe Railway Company v. White, No. 05-259, Justice Breyer said the standard the court was adopting would not impose a "general civility code" on the workplace. Rather, he said, it would serve to "screen out trivial conduct while effectively capturing those acts that are likely to dissuade employees from complaining."

Context and common sense mattered, Justice Breyer said, offering as an example a refusal by an employer to take an employee to lunch. That would usually be nothing more than a "petty slight," he said. But he added: "But to retaliate by excluding an employee from a weekly training lunch that contributes significantly to the employee's professional advancement might well deter a reasonable employee from complaining about discrimination."

The plaintiff, Ms. White, was the only woman working in the railroad's Tennessee Yard in Memphis. Because she had previous experience, she was assigned to operate a forklift, a desirable task among the jobs that "track laborers" performed. After she complained that her immediate supervisor was making inappropriate remarks, she was taken off the forklift.

Meaning of "Normal" Is at Heart of Gay Marriage Ruling

By Anemona Hartocollis
July 8, 2006

In this week's ruling against same-sex marriage in New York, judges on the Court of Appeals—those voting with the majority and those voting against it—went out of their way to compare the gay marriage movement with the struggle for civil rights by black Americans.

While the majority 4-2 decision acknowledged that gays and lesbians had suffered from discrimination, it did not see the civil rights challenges they faced, including efforts to win the right to marry, as having the same moral urgency as racial discrimination.

"Racism has been recognized for centuries—at first by a few people, and later by many more—as a revolting moral evil," wrote Judge Robert S. Smith, the author of the majority opinion. Gay marriage, on the other hand, is a relatively new concept, he wrote.

The dissenting judges said racism and discrimination against gay and lesbian people were the same. If marriage is a fundamental right, as the United States Supreme Court held in 1967 in a decision on interracial marriages, then it is a fundamental right for all individuals, the dissenters said.

Underlying the differing opinions, legal experts said, were conflicting views of what is normal and what is abnormal, with those opinions providing somewhat of a Rorschach test of each judge's individual background or experience. Yet history has shown that normality is a flexible standard, they said.

"That's the challenge that America has been struggling with since its founding, of how do we as a society deal with difference?" Victor A. Bolden, general counsel for the NAACP Legal Defense and Educational Fund, said yesterday. The fund filed a friend-of-the-court brief for the plaintiffs in the New York case.

"Do you simply give way to what the tradition is?" he asked.

Judge Smith found that restricting marriages to heterosexual couples could be justified by arguing that it promotes responsible procreation and that children are best off when they are raised by a mother and a father. He left some room for adoptive and childless heterosexual parents, to avoid "grossly intrusive inquiries" into their private lives.

He said there was little scientific evidence to support one kind of parenting over another, but the idea that a mother and a father were the best parents was supported by "intuition" and "common sense."

But gay-marriage advocates saw the rationale for limiting marriage to heterosexuals as an expression of what the majority saw as normal.

> "Times can blind us to certain truths, and later generations can see that laws once thought necessary and proper in fact serve only to oppress."

"The real point here is that the child welfare rationale is a stand-in for the majority's discomfort with gay parents," said Suzanne B. Goldberg, a clinical professor and director of the Sexuality and Gender Law Clinic at Columbia University. "But the majority couldn't have gotten away with saying that."

Professor Goldberg compared the Court of Appeals' ruling to Palmore v. Sidoti, a 1982 decision in which a Florida court held that a child of a divorced couple could be transferred from the custody of her white mother to her white father because the mother had later married a black man.

The Florida court, which was overruled in 1984 by the United States Supreme Court, said it was acting to avoid the social stigma of the child being raised in an interracial home. In that case, Professor Goldberg said, the court used the stigma as a rationale because "it couldn't get away with saying it was uncomfortable with mixed-race parents."

Yet there were those who said the majority was perfectly within its rights to make a ruling based on its concept of normality.

"Look, every social institution that matters is normative," said Monte Stewart, a lawyer and president of the Marriage Law Foundation, which opposes gay marriage. "Institutions like marriage are nothing other than shared public meanings from which arrive norms. They're trying to hijack this institution for a nonmarriage purpose, to preach the gospel that all different types of intimate adult relationships are equally valid and should be equally respected."

Time will judge who is right: Mr. Stewart and the court majority, or Chief Judge Judith S. Kaye, whose dissent quoted the Supreme Court: "Times can blind us to certain truths, and later generations can see that laws once thought necessary and proper in fact serve only to oppress."

VIII. PERSPECTIVES ON HOUSING AND HOMELESSNESS

Housing is a commodity rather than a right in America, and the harsh reality is that, for many, keeping a roof over their heads is problematic. Both the first and the fourth articles discuss recent innovations in working with the chronically homeless. Counter-intuitively, "housing first" policies seem to compare favorably with traditional approaches and do so with a lower social cost. In the second article, the redevelopment of Atlanta is seen as a classic example of the compromises involved when new housing replaces the old, and in the third article, the variety of approaches used in New York to maintain valid housing options for the working class are presented. One need look no further than these examples to conclude that market forces may be inadequate to resolve the nation's housing challenges. Is it time for a broader and more comprehensive national policy, or will the current patchwork of regulations just have to do?

As you read the following articles, consider how you would answer these questions.

30. Homelessness, Halved (02/26/06)

- Describe what "housing first" means.
- What is the traditional approach to housing for the chronically homeless?

31. Gentrification Changing Face of New Atlanta (03/11/06)

- How has gentrification changed Atlanta?
- With what has Atlanta replaced public housing?

32. Lower-Priced Housing is Vanishing at a Faster Pace (05/27/06)

- Who relies on subsidized rental apartments in New York City?
- Why is the New York City housing market called "in crisis?"

33. Homeless Alcoholics Receive a Permanent Place to Live, and Drink (07/05/06)

- Who are the "unsympathetic homeless?"
- How much money did the public spend on each homeless alcoholic in 2003?

Homelessness, Halved

By David Scharfenberg
February 26, 2006

Ravaged by crack cocaine and mental illness, Bernadette Hopson was living in a shelter here six years ago when officials with Pathways to Housing, a New York nonprofit agency, approached her with an offer she could hardly believe: an apartment and a set of keys with no strings attached.

Ms. Hopson had heard plenty of promises on the street, so she was skeptical of this one. "But Pathways wasn't like that," she said in a recent telephone interview. "They were true to their word."

In a radical departure from traditional homeless policy, Pathways does not require any of its clients to seek treatment before moving into permanent housing. In fact it does not require treatment at any point. The hope is that a home will provide the stability a client needs to make use of the job-placement, substance-abuse and mental-health services that Pathways provides.

Ms. Hopson, like many of its clients, was ready for help when approached. She had already enrolled in a drug treatment program—tired, she said, of going to sleep and waking up with a crack pipe in her mouth. And she was grateful for the psychiatric care that Pathways offered.

Now 48, she says she has been "clean and serene" for almost five years. She is attending a day program in Mount Vernon operated by the Rockland Psychiatric Center and has a part-time job as a maintenance worker with Pathways. "I'm very happy with my life now," she said.

Fifteen years ago Ms. Hopson's life would have provided a bright paragraph in an otherwise shameful tale of county homelessness on the rise. Today her case is instead a chapter in what county officials and advocates for the homeless are calling a triumphal public-policy story.

Combining rent subsidies, eviction-prevention grants and programs like Pathways, county officials and advocates say, they have cut the homeless rolls by two-thirds since Andrew J. Spano took office as county executive eight years ago. Last month 1,216 people were reported to be homeless, according to county figures, down from 3,660 in January 1998.

The sharp drop puts Westchester among a select group of cities and counties, stretching from St. Louis to San Francisco, that have begun to conquer what once seemed an intractable problem. "It's a fantastic success story," said Bob Miller, president of Westhab Inc., a homeless services agency based in Elmsford. "The rest of the country is learning now what Westchester County has done and is trying to learn some lessons."

The success, to be sure, is a qualified one. Advocates say single homeless adults do not receive the level of support afforded to families—Ms. Hopson's story notwithstanding. And programs like Pathways, which hand apartments to chronic drunks and drug addicts with little expected in return, have raised a number of sticky moral questions. But even critics acknowledge that Westchester has come a long way since the 1980's, when homelessness emerged as a serious concern here and across the nation.

Local officials' first response was to place the homeless in a series of cheap hotels and motels around the county. The move inevitably created friction with the surrounding communities; nowhere was this more evident than in the Village of Elmsford, a small, tight-knit community of blue-collar workers and professionals.

By the early 1990's the county had filled four motels along Tarrytown Road in Elmsford. And in 1991, as the homeless population was reaching its peak, the village of 3,900 had roughly 560 homeless residents. Crime surged, protesters marched and the news media deemed Elmsford the "homeless capital of Westchester."

"It got us a bad reputation," said Arthur DeAngelis, the former mayor of Elmsford. "Housing sales dropped. Nobody wanted to be here."

In 1991, the county agreed to shut three of the four hotels. But a former Howard Johnson's, converted to a full-service shelter, remained open. The Westhab Family Center, as it was called, had its successes. Katie Green, a formerly homeless mother of six, said she turned her life around there. "That's where all my miracles began," said Ms. Green, 48, who is juggling two jobs with Westhab and pursuing a bachelor's degree at the College of New Rochelle.

There were persistent complaints about loud music, drug activity and garbage tossed onto neighbors' lawns—though a shift in the shelter's security team improved the situation in 2000.

Four years later the county built a 15-foot wall along the rear of the property. George Kraemer, a biology professor at Purchase College whose property abuts the shelter, said the wall created a necessary barrier between clashing cultures. "It allowed people to move out of sight, out of mind—on both sides," he said.

These days the wall is less relevant. A week and a half ago, in a sign of the times, Westhab closed the Family Center in the face of declining homelessness. The move came just months after the county shut shelters in Yorktown and at the county airport and consolidated them at the county-owned Grasslands complex in Valhalla.

County officials and advocates ascribe the drop in homelessness, in large part, to new government policies and programs. One county-financed effort, begun in October 2000, has paid a portion of the rent for 200 working families who are homeless, or on the brink of homelessness, as they await federal housing vouchers.

Another has grown out of a series of lawsuits filed in New York and in Nassau, Suffolk and Westchester Counties in the last 20 years arguing that the state does not provide welfare recipients with enough money for housing. The cases, still continuing, helped prod the state into modest increases in the so-called "shelter allowance" in 1988 and again in 2003. The suits also contributed to a 2003 regulatory change that allows counties to seek extra funds for vulnerable populations.

The county began offering the extra money in April 2004, doubling the shelter allowance for families on welfare and making rents that once seemed out of reach suddenly more affordable. The allowance for a family of four, for instance, jumped to $958 a month from $479 a month. About 400 families have made use of the program since its inception, according to county officials.

Programs like these have stirred some controversy in public-policy circles, raising fears of dependency in an era of welfare reform. But "housing first" programs like Pathways, and a similar county initiative known as Westcares, have raised the most interesting ethical questions.

Sam Tsemberis, executive director of Pathways, started it in New York in 1992 to address the needs of the chronically homeless—that small sliver of street people who ricochet among jails, hospitals and detox centers for years on end, racking up millions of dollars in costs.

The traditional approach has been to require this population to clean itself up before obtaining housing. But the approach, however fair, does not work, Mr. Tsemberis said. "The reason that we've had this group of chronically homeless people," he said, is that officials controlling the programs are "very attached to that idea."

Thus far the Pathways alternative— providing housing first, with a team of social workers, psychiatrists, nurses, employment specialists, substance-abuse counselors and peer counselors offering support afterward—has proved effective. A federally funded study, written by Mr. Tsemberis, randomly assigned 225 homeless people to either Pathways

or New York's traditional homeless service program and tracked them for 24 months; 80 percent of Pathways clients found and maintained housing, compared with 34 percent in the control group.

The program has proved cost effective as well. In Westchester, a year of Pathways housing costs about $23,000, versus $36,000 to $48,000 a year for a shelter, according to Kevin Mahon, commissioner of the county Department of Social Services. Mr. Mahon says the county is considering a top-to-bottom shift to the housing-first model.

The effect of the approach, on both the homeless populations and the bottom line, has made it attractive to liberals and conservatives alike. The Bush administration has placed the concept at the center of its 10-year plan to end chronic homelessness.

But in Westchester, the housing-first initiative is so far one of the few new programs aimed at single homeless adults, who numbered 305 last month, according to county figures. While the county has made progress with this population, some, like Karen Fracassi, say it is not enough. "They do literally nothing to help," said Ms. Fracassi, 46, who has channeled her frustration into plans for a new nonprofit that would

The effect of the [housing first] approach, on both the homeless populations and the bottom line, has made it attractive to liberals and conservatives alike.

hire homeless people to build affordable housing.

Advocates like Paul Anderson-Winchell, executive director of Grace Church Community Center in White Plains, say the county is a long way from declaring victory over homelessness. Anyone who doubts that, he said, need only come to the center's men's shelter, where dozens of homeless people appear every day this time of year to escape the cold and eat a warm breakfast.

"We're having some successes," Mr. Anderson-Winchell said, "but the need is still immense."

Gentrification Changing Face of New Atlanta

By Shaila Dewan; Brenda Goodman, contributing reporter
March 11, 2006

In-town living. Live-work-play. Mixed income. The buzzwords of soft-core urbanism are everywhere these days in this eternally optimistic city, used in

real estate advertisements and mayoral boasts to lure money from the suburbs and to keep young people from leaving.

Loft apartments roll onto the market every week, the public housing authority is a nationally recognized pioneer in redevelopment and the newest shopping plaza has one Target and three Starbucks outlets.

But although gentrification has expanded the city's tax base and weeded out blight, it has had an unintended effect on Atlanta, long a lure to African-Americans and a symbol of black success. For the first time since the 1920's, the black share of the city's population is declining and the white percentage is on the rise.

The change has introduced an element of uncertainty into local politics, which has been dominated by blacks since 1973, when Atlanta became the first major Southern city to elect a black mayor.

Some, like Mayor Shirley Franklin, who is serving her second and final term, play down the significance of the change, saying that the city—now 54 percent black—will remain progressive and that voters here do not strictly adhere to racial lines. Others warn of the dilution, if not the demise, of black power.

"It's certainly affecting local politics," said Billy Linville, a political consultant who has worked for Ms. Franklin. "More white politicians are focusing on possibly becoming mayor and positioning themselves accordingly, whereas in the past they would not have. The next mayor of Atlanta, I believe, will be African-American, but after that it may get very interesting."

The changes do not mean that Atlanta has lost its magnetism for blacks. Twenty-year projections show the percentage of African-Americans continuing to inch upward in the 10-county metropolitan area. Blacks already hold the majority on the Clayton County commission, and they are gaining footholds in counties like Cobb and Gwinnett.

But the city itself, a small splotch of fewer than half a million residents in a galaxy of sprawl, is now attracting the affluent, who are mostly white, in part because they want to avoid gear-grinding commutes that are among the nation's longest.

In that sense, demographers say, the shift is driven by class rather than race. In 1990, the per capita income in the city of Atlanta was below that of the metropolitan area as a whole, but in 2004 it was 28 percent higher, the largest such shift in the country, according to a University of Virginia urban planning study.

So rapid is the explosion of wealth that Ms. Franklin recently tried to impose a moratorium on McMansions, new houses bloated far beyond the size of their older neighbors.

According to census figures, non-Hispanic blacks went from a high of 66.8 percent of Atlanta's population in 1990 to 61 percent in 2000 and to 54 percent in 2004. In the same time period, non-Hispanic whites went from 30.3 percent to 35 percent. The 2004 figures are estimates.

Even the Old Fourth Ward, the once elegant black neighborhood where Martin Luther King Jr. was born, is now less than 75 percent black, down from 94 percent in 1990, as houses have skyrocketed in value and low-rent apartments have been replaced by new developments.

"There could be a time in the not-too-distant future when the black population is below half of the city population, if this trend continues," said William Frey, a demographer at the Brookings Institution, a Washington research group.

Atlanta's upward shift in its white population is atypical, Mr. Frey said. Although many other cities have embarked on revitalization programs, only Washington is seeing a similar, if less stark, racial trend as Atlanta. More often, blacks and whites both are losing ground to a surging Latino population. Even in Atlanta, the Latino population rose to 26,100 in 2004 from 18,700 in 2000.

Most mayors would see a physical revitalization like Atlanta's as an accomplishment. The city has led the country, rivaled only by Chicago, in the race to replace public housing projects with mixed-income developments.

Housing has also mushroomed in places where it had not previously existed. The most ambitious project, Atlantic Station, a shopping and resi-dential district on the site of a former steel mill near downtown, will have more than 2,000 units. Loft prices start at $160,000.

But critics say Mayor Franklin and her predecessor, Bill Campbell, betrayed their voter base by not doing enough to keep Atlanta affordable for poor blacks as property taxes increase and landlords sell out to developers.

"It's clear as the nose on your face who it's going to impact the most," said Joe Beasley, the human resources director at an Atlanta church and a member of the city's Gentrification Task Force, now defunct, which studied ways to ease the effects of rising property taxes and housing prices. "Bill Campbell was cutting his own throat, and Shirley Franklin is continuing to cut her own throat."

Ms. Franklin counters that many new developments, including Atlantic Station, have set aside areas for low-income or affordable housing. She says one of her major accomplishments, financing a badly needed overhaul of the sewage and water system without a large increase in rates, has kept city living affordable. But the bottom line, in the mayor's view, is that the city must try to mold development where it can.

"We're constantly seeking a balance in what we support," Ms. Franklin said last week in a telephone interview.

David Bositis, a senior political analyst at the Joint Center for Political and Economic Studies, a Washington group that studies black issues, said he viewed the change as largely positive. "I don't know that it ever was a good thing when you had cities that were becoming viewed as black cities," Mr. Bositis said.

He added, "People said, 'This is our city now,' but half the time you looked at what was there and you said, 'Who cares?'"

Race is not the only factor in the political equation.

"We're talking about an era in which you see a conservative trend among certain sectors of the black community,"

The changes do not mean that Atlanta has lost its magnetism for blacks.

said William Boone, a political science professor at Clark Atlanta University, a predominantly African-American institution. "That's going to have some impact on who's offered for mayor."

Power in Atlanta has always involved coalitions of blacks and other groups, said Ms. Franklin, who has received high marks for restoring credibility to city government and who was re-elected in 2005 with 91 percent of the vote.

"This whole notion that the sky is falling, I don't see it," Ms. Franklin said. "To me the question is, Will Atlanta be a progressive city, given that it's the home of the civil rights movement, the home of the historically black colleges? Will that continue with the demographic shifts? And my answer is yes."

Already, the change has had unpredictable effects. Kwanza Hall is a young black politician from the rapidly gentrifying Old Fourth Ward, a neighborhood that is part of a mostly white City Council district that includes affluent areas like Inman Park. But in the last election, Mr. Hall, who ran his campaign from a year-old coffee shop next to a soon-to-open men's spa, defeated two whites for an open seat.

To Joe Stewardson, who owns the coffee shop building and was the first white president of the ward's community development corporation, the question was not Mr. Hall's race but his ability to forge relationships outside a neighborhood whose boundary was, not too long ago, what Mr. Stewardson called "an iron curtain."

"You would not have seen that," Mr. Stewardson said, "if this neighborhood had not changed so much."

Lower-Priced Housing Is Vanishing at a Faster Pace

By Janny Scott
May 27, 2006

The shrinking of New York City's supply of privately owned but subsidized rental apartments—housing relied upon by many working-class New Yorkers as well as teachers, civil servants and police officers—has accelerated sharply over the past three years, according to two new studies tracking the erosion of lower-priced housing in the city.

A study to be released today by the Community Service Society of New York found that nearly a quarter of the roughly 121,000 apartments built under federal and state subsidy programs dating from the 1960's and 1970's left those programs from 1990 to 2005. The rate of withdrawal grew in the late 1990's and hit its highest level last year.

Another study, released on Thursday by the Office of the New York City Comptroller looked largely at losses from the state's Mitchell-Lama program, and found that more than 25,000 units have been withdrawn or have begun that process since 2004. That number is greater than the 24,000 units pulled out in all the years before 2004, the study said.

"When we last looked in 2003, an estimated 10 percent of the stock was lost or in the process," said Victor Bach, the senior housing policy analyst at the Community Service Society and an author of its report, along with Tom Waters. "Now it's up to 25 percent. It's really accelerating."

Both reports suggested that the losses may soon outweigh the effects of Mayor Michael R. Bloomberg's efforts to build and preserve 165,000 units of low- and moderate-income housing by 2013. But city officials said the 56,000 units that they say the administration has already financed significantly exceeds the number of units lost.

They also said many residents of buildings have been able to remain in their buildings without paying high rents. Buildings built before 1974 fall under the rent stabilization system, and tenants in other buildings get federal Section 8 vouchers, which cover the gap between the rent they can afford and the market rate.

"That's not to say this is not an issue, that we shouldn't do more," Shaun Donovan, commissioner of the city's Department of Housing Preservation and Development, said of the reports. "But I think they're overstating what the impact is."

According to city figures, there are about 250,000 units of government-assisted housing in the city, developed through low-income housing tax credits, the Mitchell-Lama program and various federal subsidy programs. Under Mitchell-Lama and similar programs, in return for the government aid, building owners were required to keep rents affordable to low- and moderate-income people for a time, often 20 years, before they could leave the programs.

In recent years, more buildings have become eligible to withdraw. The strength of the real estate market has created new incentives to pull out. The Bloomberg administration, with some success, has developed programs to encourage owners to stay, but attrition has continued.

"Since 2004, the number has skyrocketed," said William C. Thompson Jr., the city comptroller, citing his office's study of losses of units from the Mitchell-Lama program and the similar Limited Dividend housing program. "In 2004, what we had talked about was an impending crisis in affordable housing. Today, that crisis is here."

The Community Service Society study looked at losses not only from the

Mitchell-Lama program, but also from two federal mortgage-interest subsidy programs and the project-based Section 8 rent subsidy program. The study found that 23 percent of 120,917 apartments were lost from 1990 to 2005, including 5,518 in 2005 alone. Another 13 percent are imminently at risk, it said.

Attrition has been heaviest among Mitchell-Lama apartments, Mr. Waters said. Just 1,111 Mitchell-Lama apartments with a federal subsidy had been lost through 2002; by early this year, that number had risen to 9,528. Among those without a federal subsidy, 12,755, or 53 percent of all units, were lost from 1990 to 2005.

The number lost from the project-based Section 8 program rose to 5,478 in late 2005 from 3,363 in 2002.

The comptroller's office found that 28 Mitchell-Lama developments and one Limited Dividend development, totaling 13,000 units, have begun withdrawing. It predicted that if they withdraw, the city will have lost 49,000 units, or 33 percent of all units built under those two programs.

The comptroller's office calculated that the city had financed the creation of 12,229 low and moderate-income units in the period since 2002, a period in which the study said 12,943 Mitchell-Lama units were lost. But city officials said they have financed the preservation and creation of over 56,000 low- and middle-income units since 2002.

Mr. Waters said he did not think that the losses have outweighed the gains in lower-priced housing yet but they could do so in the future. He said that a lot of the new units being created by the city

> *"Because of how much of your income you spend just renting an apartment, you can't really live a decent life or really enjoy all the offers and benefits the city has."*

are for middle-income people—out of reach of many in the group that the older subsidized apartments have tended to house.

Among other recommendations, the Community Service Society called for federal funding to increase the subsidy for projects in areas in which the real estate market is hot, state help in refinancing mortgages, and improved tenant protections. Both studies urged the State Legislature to pass two pending bills that would place all Mitchell-Lama rental buildings under rent stabilization once they leave the program.

Interviews with tenants in several buildings that have left the subsidy programs indicated that change has been gradual in many cases.

Jean Green Dorsey, chairwoman of the tenants association in an Upper West Side apartment complex that left the Mitchell-Lama program eight years ago, said more than 80 percent of tenants have stayed and are paying rents at the stabilized rate. Mrs. Dorsey, who said that she and her husband pay $600 for their two-bedroom apartment with a terrace, said that rents for vacant apartments have tripled.

Edward Clarke, president of the tenants association at Boulevard Towers I in Soundview in the Bronx, which also left Mitchell-Lama, said tenants who stayed are paying rents similar to what they paid before. But, he said, evictions have gone up. And, in 10 years, he predicts, the residents will be a different crowd.

"Quite frankly, a lot of people I know are moving out of the city altogether," said Mr. Clarke, 36, an operations analyst with Mellon Investor Services. "Because of how much of your income you spend just renting an apartment, you can't really live a decent life or really enjoy all the offers and benefits the city has."

Homeless Alcoholics Receive a Permanent Place to Live, and Drink

By Jessica Kowal
July 5, 2006
(Correction Appended)

SEATTLE, JUNE 30—Rodney Littlebear was a homeless drunk who for 15 years ran up the public tab with trips to jail, homeless shelters and emergency rooms.

He now has a brand-new, government-financed apartment where he can drink as much as he wants. It is part of a first-in-the-nation experiment to ease the torment of drug and alcohol addiction while saving taxpayers' money.

Last year, King County created a list of 200 "chronic public inebriates" in the Seattle region who had cost the most to round up and care for. Seventy-five were offered permanent homes in a new apartment building known by its address, 1811 Eastlake.

Each had been a street drunk for several years and had failed at least six efforts at sobriety. In a controversial acknowledgment of their addiction, the residents—70 men and 5 women—can drink in their rooms. They do not have to promise to drink less, attend Alcoholics Anonymous or go to church.

"They woke me up in detox and told me they were going to move me in," said Mr. Littlebear, 37, who has had a series of strokes and uses a walker. "When I got here, I said, 'Oh boy, this don't look like no treatment center.'"

These are the "unsympathetic homeless" who beg, drink, urinate and vomit in public— and they are probably the most difficult to get off the streets, said Bill Hobson, executive director of the Downtown Emergency Service Center, the nonprofit group that owns 1811 Eastlake.

In 2003, the public spent $50,000, on average, for each of 40 homeless alcoholics found most often at the jail, the sobering center and the public Harborview Medical Center, said Amnon Shoenfeld, director of King County's division of mental health and chemical abuse.

Mr. Hobson's group expected the annual cost for each new resident of 1811 Eastlake to be $13,000, or a total of $950,000. It cost $11.2 million to build and is paid for entirely by the City of Seattle and county, state and federal governments.

The actual price tag will probably rise because residents have more serious health problems than expected, said Margaret King, a social worker who manages the building. Many have heart ailments, cirrhosis, diabetes, head injuries from falling on sidewalks and severe circulation problems. Four residents have already died, including one who moved in with late-stage liver cancer.

The building's critics are particularly incensed that residents do not have to stay sober. The Seattle Times, in 2004, editorialized that government should insist that the residents quit drinking in order to live there.

"Bunks for drunks—it's a living monument to failed social policy," said John Carlson, a conservative radio talk show host here. This approach, he said, is "aiding and abetting someone's self-destruction."

Drink they do. When residents are shuttled to supermarkets for groceries, Ms. King said, they often buy wine or beer, which is sold in this state alongside the milk, eggs and orange juice.

Like Mr. Littlebear, Howard Hunt, 41, moved in the first day. Homeless since 1999, Mr. Hunt said he drank a daily bottle of whiskey before he came to 1811 Eastlake. He has epilepsy and walks with crutches because he fractured his hip.

He shrugged when asked about the policy allowing him to drink in his new home. "We're going to drink somewhere," Mr. Hunt said.

Influential Bush administration officials have come to support this project, including the on-site drinking. John Meyers, director of the Department of Housing and Urban Development's regional office here, said he blanched when he learned that his agency had pledged $2 million for it. He now calls 1811 Eastlake "a glorious experiment."

"It's a lot cheaper having them spend the night at 1811 than at the E.R. or at the drunk tank," Mr. Meyers said.

Philip F. Mangano, executive director of the United States Interagency Council on Homelessness, said there should be a similar building in every city in the country.

These apartments fit into the "housing first" philosophy, newly adopted by many cities, intended to give permanent housing and intensive services to long-term homeless people. Local officials have already approved other buildings for the mentally ill and people with chronic medical conditions, said Adrienne Quinn, director of Seattle's Housing Office.

"It's a lot cheaper having them spend the night at 1811 than at the E.R. or at the drunk tank."

Though it would be unthinkable for a market-rate apartment building in this booming city, 1811 Eastlake's front door is across the street from busy Interstate 5, on the edge of downtown. The Starbucks around the corner donates pastries, but Robb Anderson, 43, an owner of the trophy shop next door to the apartments, complained bitterly about paramedics' 120 visits in just six months.

The building's atmosphere during a recent daytime visit was more convalescent home than rowdy dorm. A few men in the television room stared silently at a World Cup match, while others wearing backpacks trudged through the front door and into the communal kitchen for apple fritters and coffee.

A third of the residents, including Mr. Littlebear, are American Indian; an estimated 20 percent are military veterans. The average age is 45. Most receive state or federal disability payments, and all residents pay 30 percent of their income as rent under HUD's guideline for low-income housing.

By choice or if they need frequent medical attention, 26 residents live on the first floor in office-sized cubicles with a bed, desk, dresser and small refrigerator. These communal living areas have a strong scent of body odor.

Upstairs, 49 people have private studio apartments with a single bed, bath and kitchen. For many, this normal existence is a huge adjustment. One man continues to sleep on the floor next to his bed, and another refused sheets in favor of his sleeping bag, Ms. King said.

Their quality of life, drinking and use of public services are being studied by researchers at the University of Washington. Ms. King said the alcohol intake of the residents was shockingly high at first, but many residents say they now drink less, at least by their standards.

"I cut down," Mr. Littlebear said. "I've got to save my liver."

■ **Correction:** July 12, 2006. An article on July 5 about an apartment building for homeless alcoholics in Seattle referred incompletely to its financing. Private sector investors, who receive federal tax credits, contributed to the cost of the building; it was not solely financed with government funds.

IX. PERSPECTIVES ON INCOME DISPARITIES

The rich keep on getting richer in America. While some degree of inequality may actually result in economic advance by providing more incentive to work harder and smarter, there are distinct dangers as well. The first article presents a few possibilities. But income disparities between rich and poor are not the only income gaps in America. The second article highlights the challenges facing younger workers, especially the income gap between those with a college education and those without. The third article discusses some of the many aspects influencing racial income disparities, but we return to the rich/poor divide again in the last article. When is income disparity too wide? When does redistribution become appropriate?

As you read the following articles, consider how you would answer these questions.

34. Economic View: Income Inequality, and Its Cost (06/25/06)

- What are the adverse effects of inequality?
- How does inequality "lower productivity and weaken inefficiency"?

35. Many Entry-Level Workers Feel Pinch of Rough Market (09/04/06)

- Are entry level wages increasing or decreasing for the high school and college educated?
- What is the size of the income gap between the high school and college educated?

36. In Queens, Blacks Are the Have-Nots No More (10/01/06)

- What is unusual about the incomes of black and white households in Queens?
- How does immigration influence the income gap in Queens?

37. Economic View: If All the Slices Are Equal, Will the Pie Shrink? (11/19/06)

- How does the recent MIT study justify the extravagantly high salaries of today's CEO's?
- What are some of the social dangers of wide income disparities?

Economic View: Income Inequality, and Its Cost

By Anna Bernasek
June 25, 2006

Inequality has always been part of the American economy, but the gap between the rich and the poor has recently been widening at an alarming rate. Today, more than 40 percent of total income is going to the wealthiest 10 percent, their biggest share of the nation's pie in at least 65 years. The social and political repercussions of this disparity have been widely debated, but what about the effects on the economy?

Oddly, despite its position in the political debate, the question has received little attention from economists. Mostly, they have focused on measuring income inequality and establishing its causes. Some research has been done, however, and the results, including insights from related disciplines like psychology and political science, are disturbing.

Start with recent findings in the field of public health. Some scientists believe that growing inequality leads to more health problems in the overall population—a situation that can reduce workers' efficiency and increase national spending on health, diverting resources away from productive endeavors like saving and investment.

Sir Michael Marmot, a professor of epidemiology and public health at University College London and director of its International Institute for Society and Health, has spent most of his career studying the link between inequality and health around the world. In a much-publicized paper published in May in The Journal of the American Medical Association, Sir Michael and three colleagues studied health in the United States and in Britain. They found that at various points throughout the social hierarchy, there was more illness in the United States than in Britain.

Sir Michael theorizes that a reason for the disparity was the greater inequalities in the United States and heavier stresses resulting from them.

Other researchers have focused on how income inequality can breed corruption. That may be especially true in democracies, where wealth and political power can be more easily exchanged, according to a study of 129 countries by Jong-Sung You, a graduate student at the Kennedy School of Government at Harvard, and Sanjeev Khagram, a professor of public affairs at the University of Washington in Seattle.

Corruption, of course, can hurt growth by reducing the efficient allocation of public and private resources and by distorting investment. That may end up creating asset price bubbles.

Unchecked inequality may also tend to create still more inequality. Edward L. Glaeser, a professor of economics at Harvard, argues that as the rich become richer and acquire greater political influence, they may support policies that make themselves even wealthier at the expense of others. In a paper published last July, he said, "If the rich can influence political outcomes through lobbying activities or membership in special interest groups, then more inequality could lead to less redistribution rather than more."

In the United States, there is plenty of evidence that this has been occurring. Bush administration policies that have already reduced the estate tax and cut the top income and capital gains tax rates benefit the well-to-do. It seems hardly an accident that the gap between rich and poor has widened.

There may be other ways in which growing inequality hurts the economy. Steven Pressman, professor of economics at Monmouth University in West Long Branch, N.J., has identified a psychological effect that may lower productivity and reduce efficiency. Professor Pressman draws on the work of Daniel Kahneman, a Nobel laureate in economics, and his experiments on fairness. One experiment, called the ultimatum game, involves two people with a fixed sum of money that must be divided between them. One person is to propose any division he likes; the other can only accept or reject it. If the division is accepted, each person receives the proposed amount; if it is rejected, neither gets anything.

It might be expected that a rational individual in the role of divider would take a large part of the money and that rational receivers would accept a small portion rather than walk away with nothing. But it turned out that when faced with an offer they considered unfair, most people rejected it outright. Perhaps in anticipation of this, many dividers made substantial offers.

Professor Pressman relates those results to economic behavior in corporate America. "If a C.E.O.'s salary is going through the roof and workers are getting pay cuts, what will happen?" he said. "Workers can't outright reject the offer—they need to work—but they can reject it by working less hard and not caring about the quality of what they are producing. Then the whole efficiency of the firm is affected."

> *Current policies appear to be worsening the situation.*

The effects of income inequality aren't entirely negative. Without some inequality, there would be little economic incentive to earn more. And some researchers, particularly advocates of supply-side theories, predict that as the rich get richer, their increased wealth will be used for greater savings and investment, thereby bolstering growth. The latest data on the American economy, though, do not seem to support this prediction.

Savings among top income earners have actually declined. According to the Federal Reserve's latest Survey of Consumer Finance, the percentage of families in the top 10 percent by income that saved anything at all dropped to 80.6 percent in 2004 from 84.3 percent in 2001. And this was during a period when President Bush cut top marginal income tax rates and taxes on capital gains and dividends.

The trend of growing income inequality may eventually be reversed, but at the moment, current policies appear to be worsening the situation. If more researchers turned their attention to the subject, they would find plenty to explore.

Many Entry-Level Workers Feel Pinch of Rough Market

By Steven Greenhouse
September 4, 2006

This Labor Day, the 45 million young people in the nation's work force face a choppy job market in which entry-level wages have often trailed inflation, making it hard for many to cope with high housing costs and rising college debt loads.

Entry-level wages for college and high school graduates fell by more than 4 percent from 2001 to 2005, after factoring in inflation, according to an analysis of Labor Department data by the Economic Policy Institute. In addition, the percentage of college graduates receiving health and pension benefits in their entry-level jobs has dropped sharply.

Some labor experts say wage stagnation and the sharp increase in housing costs over the past decade have delayed workers ages 20 to 35 from buying their first homes.

"People are getting married later, they're having children later, and they're buying houses later," said Cecilia E. Rouse, an economist at Princeton University and a co-editor of a forthcoming book on the economics of early adulthood. "There's been a lengthening of the transition to adulthood, and it is very possible that what has happened in the economy is leading to some of these changes."

Census Bureau data released last week underlined the difficulties for young workers, showing that median income for families with at least one parent age 25 to 34 fell $3,009 from 2000 to 2005, sliding to $48,405, a 5.9 percent drop, after having jumped 12 percent in the late 1990's.

Worsening the financial crunch, far more college graduates are borrowing to pay for their education, and the amount borrowed has jumped by more than 50 percent in recent years, largely because of soaring tuition.

In 2004, 50 percent of graduating seniors borrowed some money for college, with their debt load averaging $19,000, Dr. Rouse said. That was a sharp increase from 1993, when 35 percent of seniors borrowed for college and their debt averaged $12,500, in today's dollars.

Even though the economy has grown strongly in recent years, wages for young workers, especially college graduates, have been depressed by several factors, including the end of the high-tech boom and the trend of sending jobs overseas. From 2001 to 2005, entry-level wages for male college graduates fell by 7.3 percent, to $19.72 an hour, while wages for female graduates declined 3.5 percent, to $17.08, according to the Economic Policy Institute, a liberal research group.

"In a weak labor market, younger workers do the worst," said Lawrence Mishel, the institute's president. "Young workers are on the cutting edge of experiencing all the changes in the economy."

Lawrence F. Katz, a labor economist at Harvard, said plenty of slack remained in the job market for young workers.

The percentage of young adults who are working has dropped since 2000 largely because many have grown discouraged and stopped looking for work. This has happened even though the unemployment rate, which counts only people looking for work, has fallen to 4.4 percent for those ages 25 to 34. It is 8.2 percent for workers ages 20 to 24.

"Any way you slice the data, the labor market has been pretty weak the past five years," Dr. Katz said. "But hotshot young people coming out of top universities have done fine, just like top-notch executives have."

In a steep drop over a short time, 64 percent of college graduates received health coverage in entry-level jobs in 2005, down from 71 percent five years earlier. As employers grapple with fast-rising health costs, many companies have reduced health coverage, with those cutbacks sharpest among young workers.

Partly because of the decline in manufacturing jobs that were a ticket to middle-class life, just one-third of workers with high school diplomas receive health coverage in entry-level jobs, down from two-thirds in 1979.

After an extensive job search, Katey Rich, who graduated from Wesleyan University in June, landed a part-time, $14-an-hour job in Manhattan as an editorial assistant at Film Journal International. With one-bedroom apartments often renting for $2,000 a month, Ms. Rich is looking to share an apartment but is staying with a friend's parents for now. And while she is excited about her new job, she said she was concerned that it did not come with health insurance.

"I'll have to fend for myself," said Ms. Rich, who is from Aiken, S.C. "I have parents who will back me up if things get really rough."

Mark Zandi, chief economist at Moody's Economy.com, said it was surprising how deeply young workers were going into debt to maintain the living standards they want.

"The post-boomer generation feels very cavalier about saving," Mr. Zandi said. "They've been very aggressively dis-saving and have borrowed significantly."

John Arnold, 28, a materials-handling specialist at a Caterpillar factory in Morton, Ill., said he was having a hard time making ends meet. At his factory, Caterpillar has pressured the union to accept a two-tier contract in which newer workers like him will earn a maximum of $13.26 an hour—$27,000 a year for a full-time worker—no matter how long they work. For longtime Caterpillar workers in the upper tier, the wage ceiling is often $20 or more an hour.

"A few people I work with are living at home with their parents; some are even on food stamps," said Mr. Arnold, a Caterpillar worker for seven years. "I was hoping to buy a house this year, but there's just no way I can swing it." With just a high school diploma, he said it was hard to find jobs that paid more.

For men with high school diplomas, entry-level pay fell by 3.3 percent, to $10.93, from 2001 to 2005, according to the Economic Policy Institute. For

"The future is bright for young people because the opportunities are out there," said Mason Bishop, deputy assistant labor secretary for employment and training. "We want to help them get access to the postsecondary education that enables them to take advantage of the opportunities."

The wage gap between college-educated and high-school-educated workers has widened greatly, with college graduates earning 45 percent more than high school graduates, up from 23 percent in 1979.

Professor Rouse of Princeton said a college degree added $402,000 to a graduate's lifetime earnings.

Alex Shayevsky, who graduated from New York University last year, said majoring in business had paid off. Mr. Shayevsky got a job in the bond department of a major investment bank in New York. He earns $65,000, not including a bonus that could be at least half his salary.

"Getting my degree was very valuable," said Mr. Shayevsky, a 23-year-old from Buffalo Grove, Ill.

Martin Regalia, chief economist for the United States Chamber of Commerce, said young workers would be helped greatly if strong economic growth continued and the labor market tightened further, as happened in the late 1990's.

Sheldon H. Danziger, a professor of public policy at the University of Michigan, sees a bifurcated labor market for young workers.

"You're much better off as a young worker today if you're the child of the well-to-do and you get a good education," Professor Danziger said, "and you're much worse off if you're a child of a blue-collar worker and you don't go to college. There's increasing inequality among young people just as there is increasing inequality among their parents."

"You're much better off as a young worker today if you're the child of the well-to-do and you get a good education, and you're much worse off if you're a child of a blue-collar worker and you don't go to college."

The nation's personal savings sank below zero last year for the first time since the Depression, meaning Americans spent more than they earned. But for households under 35, the saving rate has plunged to minus 16 percent, which means they are spending 16 percent more than they are earning.

female high school graduates, entry-level pay fell by 4.9 percent, to $9.08 an hour.

Labor Department officials voiced optimism for young workers, noting that the Bureau of Labor Statistics had projected that 18.9 million net new jobs would be created by 2014.

In Queens, Blacks Are the Have-Nots No More

By Sam Roberts
October 1, 2006

Across the country, the income gap between blacks and whites remains wide, and nowhere more so than in Manhattan. But just a river away, a very different story is unfolding.

In Queens, the median income among black households, nearing $52,000 a year, has surpassed that of whites in 2005, an analysis of new census data shows. No other county in the country with a population over 65,000 can make that claim. The gains among blacks in Queens, the city's quintessential middle-class borough, were driven largely by the growth of two-parent families and the successes of immigrants from the West Indies. Many live in tidy homes in verdant enclaves like Cambria Heights, Rosedale and Laurelton, just west of the Cross Island Parkway and the border with Nassau County.

David Veron, a 45-year-old lawyer, is one of them. He estimates that the

now maturing and reaching the peak of our earning capacity."

Richard P. Nathan, co-director of the Nelson A. Rockefeller Institute of Government in Albany, called Queens "the flip side of the underclass."

"It really is the best illustration that the stereotype of blacks living in dangerous, concentrated, poor, slum, urban neighborhoods is misleading and doesn't predominate," he said.

Andrew A. Beveridge, a Queens College demographer who analyzed results of the Census Bureau's 2005 American Community Survey, released in August, for The New York Times, said of the trend: "It started in the early 1990's, and now it's consolidated. They're married-couple families living the American dream in southeast Queens."

In 1994, an analysis for The Times found that in some categories, the median income of black households in

the national median income, about $46,000.

Even as blacks have surged ahead of whites in Queens, over all they have fallen behind in Manhattan. With the middle class there shrinking, those remaining are largely either the wealthy, who are predominantly white, or the poor, who are mostly black and Hispanic, the new census data shows.

Median income among blacks in Manhattan was $28,116, compared with $86,494 among whites, the widest gap of any large county in the country.

In contrast, the middle-class black neighborhoods of Queens evoke the "zones of emergence" that nurtured economically rising European immigrants a century ago, experts say. "It's how the Irish, the Italians, the Jews got out of the slums," Professor Nathan said.

Despite the economic progress among blacks in Queens, income gaps still endure within the borough's black community, where immigrants, mostly from the Caribbean, are generally doing better than American-born blacks.

"Racism and the lack of opportunity created a big gap and kind of put us at a deeper disadvantage," said Steven Dennison, an American-born black resident of Springfield Gardens.

Mr. Dennison, a 49-year-old electrical contractor, has four children. One is getting her doctoral degree; another will graduate from college this school year. "It starts with the school system," Mr. Dennison said.

Mr. Vernon, the lawyer from Jamaica, said: "It's just that the people who left the Caribbean to come here are self-starters. It only stands to reason they would be more aggressive in pursuing their goals. And that creates a separation."

"They're married-couple families living the American dream in southeast Queens."

house in St. Albans that he bought with his wife, Nitchel, three years ago for about $320,000 has nearly doubled in value since they renovated it. Two-family homes priced at $600,000 and more seem to be sprouting on every vacant lot, he says.

"Southeast Queens, especially, had a heavy influx of West Indian folks in the late 80's and early 90's," said Mr. Veron, who, like his 31-year-old wife, was born on the island of Jamaica. "Those individuals came here to pursue an opportunity, and part of that opportunity was an education," he said. "A large percentage are college graduates. We're

Queens was slightly higher than that of whites—a milestone in itself. By 2000, whites had pulled slightly ahead. But blacks have since rebounded.

The only other places where black household income is higher than among whites are much smaller than Queens, like Mount Vernon in Westchester, Pembroke Pines, Fla.; Brockton, Mass.; and Rialto, Calif. Most of the others also have relatively few blacks or are poor.

But Queens is unique not only because it is home to about two million people, but also because both blacks and whites there make more than

Housing patterns do, too. While blacks make more than whites—even those in the borough's wealthiest neighborhoods, including Douglaston—they account for fewer than 1 in 20 residents in some of those communities. And among blacks themselves, there are disparities, depending on where they live.

According to the latest analysis, black households in Queens reported a median income of $51,836 compared with $50,960 for non-Hispanic whites (and $52,998 for Asians and $43,927 among Hispanic people).

Among married couples in Queens, the gap was even greater: $78,070 among blacks, higher than any other racial or ethnic group, and $74,503 among whites.

Hector Ricketts, 50, lives with his wife, Opal, a legal secretary, and their three children in Rosedale. A Jamaican immigrant, he has a master's degree in health care administration, but after he was laid off more than a decade ago he realized that he wanted to be an entrepreneur. He established a commuter van service.

"When immigrants come here, they're not accustomed to social programs," he said, "and when they see opportunities they had no access to—tuition or academic or practical training—they are God-sent, and they use those programs to build themselves and move forward."

Immigrants helped propel the gains among blacks. The median income of foreign-born black households was $61,151, compared with $45,864 for American-born blacks. The disparity was even more pronounced among black married couples.

The median for married black immigrants was $84,338, nearly as much as for native-born white couples. For married American-born blacks, it was $70,324.

One reason for the shifting income pattern is that some wealthier whites have moved away.

"As non-Hispanic whites have gotten richer, they have left Queens for the Long Island suburbs, leaving behind just middle-class whites," said Professor Edward N. Wolff, an economist at New York University. "Since home ownership is easier for whites than blacks in the suburbs—mortgages are easier to get for whites—the middle-class whites left in Queens have been relatively poor. Middle-class black families have had a harder time buying homes in the Long Island suburbs, so that blacks that remain in Queens are relatively affluent."

The white median also appeared to have been depressed slightly by the disproportionate number of elderly whites on fixed incomes.

But even among the elderly, blacks fared better. Black households headed by a person older than 65 reported a median income of $35,977, compared with $28,232 for white households.

Lloyd Hicks, 77, who moved to Cambria Heights from Harlem in 1959, used to run a freight-forwarding business near Kennedy Airport. His wife, Elvira, 71, was a teacher. Both were born in New York City, but have roots in Trinidad. He has a bachelor's degree in business. She has a master's in education.

"Education was always something the families from the islands thought the children should have," Mr. Hicks said.

In addition to the larger share of whites who are elderly, said Andrew Hacker, a Queens College political scientist, "black Queens families usually need two earners to get to parity with working whites."

Kenneth C. Holder, 46, a former prosecutor who was elected to a Civil Court judgeship last year, was born in London of Jamaican and Guyanese parents and grew up in Laurelton. His wife, Sharon, who is Guyanese, is a secretary at a Manhattan law firm. They own a home in Rosedale, where they live with their three sons.

"Queens has a lot of good places to live; I could move, but why?" Mr. Holder said. "There are quite a number of two-parent households and a lot of ancillary services available for youth, put up by organized block associations and churches, like any middle-class area."

In smaller categories, the numbers become less precise. Still, for households headed by a man, median income was $61,151 for blacks and $54,537 for whites. Among households headed by a woman, the black and white medians were the same: $50,960.

Of the more than 800,000 households in Queens, according to the Census Bureau's 2005 American Community Survey, about 39 percent are white, 23 percent are Hispanic, 18 percent are Asian, and 17 percent are black—suggesting multiple hues rather than monotone black and white.

"It is wrong to say that America is 'fast becoming two nations' the way the Kerner Commission did," said Professor Nathan, who was the research director for the National Advisory Commission on Civil Disorders in 1968 and disagreed with its conclusion. "It might be, though, that it was more true then than it is now."

Economic View: If All the Slices Are Equal, Will the Pie Shrink?

By Eduardo Porter
November 19, 2006

The chief executive of Wal-Mart Stores, H. Lee Scott Jr., made more than $15 million last year in cash, stock and options, according to the company's annual report, an amount equivalent to roughly 850 times the pay of Wal-Mart's average "associate" tending to shoppers on a superstore floor.

Mr. Scott isn't even at the top of the income-disparity league. Bruce E. Karatz, the former chief executive of the homebuilder KB Home, made $150 million last year, according to the Corporate Library, a research firm. According to government statistics, a

said Lawrence Katz, an economist at Harvard. "If you're just talking about making the pie as big as we could, it is not clear what level of inequality is best."

Like any other difference in prices, economists say, income inequality allows people and companies to better allocate investments of money and effort. Pay differences encourage the best and brightest into the most profitable lines of work, and the most profitable companies to hire them. Inequality, according to this view, provides an incentive to work extra hard to come out on top.

produce wealth, Mr. Gabaix said. "Optimal inequality is whatever the market dictates at any given time," he said. Put differently, efforts to share the pie in a more egalitarian way may reduce the size of the pastry.

In their study, Mr. Saez and Mr. Piketty found that recent growth has been faster in countries where the share of income going to the wealthy has increased sharply, including the United States, Britain and Canada, than it has in more egalitarian nations like France or Japan.

"In recent decades it looks like the link is true," Mr. Saez said. Still, the breakneck speed at which America's richest have increased their take of the economy since the 1980s is disconcerting to many analysts.

Many are skeptical that the chasm between the rewards of the rich and the rest needs to be quite so big to spur the economy along.

Half of the income gains derived from the increase in productivity from 1966 to 2001 accrued to the top 10 percent of earners.

residential construction worker makes less than one four-thousandth of that.

Executives are gorging themselves across the economy. In a study published this year, the economists Emmanuel Saez of the University of California, Berkeley, and Thomas Piketty of the École Normale Supérieure in Paris reported that the top 0.1 percent of Americans in income receive nearly 7 percent of the total, the highest share since the 1920s.

Yet while the chasm between the lavish pay packages dished out in America's executive suites and the wages of the minions below may jar archetypal notions of fairness, economists point out that not all inequality is bad. While it may have nasty side effects, some inequality is needed to spur growth.

"Clearly, perfect egalitarianism wouldn't lead to much effort or output,"

In a recent study that caused a bit of a stir in academia, two young economists, Xavier Gabaix of the Massachusetts Institute of Technology and Augustin Landier of the Leonard N. Stern School of Business at New York University, argued that the fast climb in pay for corporate chief executives had simply followed the rise in the size of American companies.

The difference in talent between the No. 1 and the No. 150 executive might not amount to much, but when the companies for which they work are humongous, these tiny differences could translate into real money. As they have grown, America's corporate behemoths have bid up the price of executives in their quest to get the best.

Matching the best executives with companies that can profit most from them, and thus pay them the most, will

"If the growth in inequality is just about improving incentives, it's gone beyond what looks necessary," Mr. Katz said. "I don't think the added incentive of earning $100 million over $50 million is very different than the incentive of making $10 million over $5 million."

Mr. Saez pointed out that Japan's postwar economic boom, which lasted until 1990, wasn't hurt by the country's relatively homogeneous income distribution. Mr. Katz noted that the United States economy grew very quickly from 1947 to 1970, a period when the distribution of rewards was much more egalitarian than it is today.

Moreover, the growing gap between rich and poor has costs that may be harder to quantify.

To begin with, growing inequality will strike many as unfair, prompting social tensions. But there are worries beyond fears of unrest. The growing share of income devoted to those at the top is leaving less and less to share among the rest of us.

In one recent study, Robert Gordon and Ian Dew-Becker, economists at Northwestern University, found that half of the income gains derived from the increase in productivity from 1966 to 2001 accrued to the top 10 percent of earners. The wages of typical American workers, meanwhile, barely grew at all.

A shrinking share of the nation's economic spoils will not only reduce workers' stake in the current social setup; it will leave them with few resources for investment in economically crucial items like education. Rising inequality will also hamper teamwork. And it may ultimately destroy incentives. If the rewards of economic growth are monopolized by the very top earners,

the rest of us may find little reason to make an effort.

Using a golf metaphor, Richard Freeman, an economist at Harvard and the National Bureau of Economic Research, said, "If Tiger won everything, nobody would want to play."

And if extreme income disparities produce anomie at the bottom, they can have even more perverse effects on the incentives at the top. For instance, those who benefit most from the current system will be tempted to help friendly politicians win elections to ensure that future economic arrangements still go their way. And, as has been shown by the run of shenanigans from the creative earnings management practiced by Enron and WorldCom a few years ago through the recently discovered backdating of options, some executives will simply cheat.

Mr. Freeman and Alexander Gelber, a Ph.D. candidate in economics

at Harvard, recently ran an experiment to figure out how inequality affects workers' efforts. They gave three groups of participants puzzles to solve and rewarded them in different ways.

The first group, in which everyone received the same reward, regardless of performance, didn't solve many puzzles. The group in which the best maze solver got all of the rewards—and no one else got anything—didn't do too much better. The group that had a sliding scale of rewards, based on performance, did the best.

Yet the most interesting result of Mr. Freeman's experiment was not about maximizing output. In an unexpected twist, some subjects of the test found ways to rig the system. Few did so when the rewards were spread in an egalitarian way. But when the rewards gave participants an incentive to compete, they also provided a powerful inducement to cheat.

X. PERSPECTIVES ON THE WAR ON DRUGS

The War on Drugs may well be the least popular federal policy. As the first article explains, despite massive resources devoted to eradication and interdiction efforts, the change in the street price, quality, and availability of drugs in America is debatable. There is little debate, however, over the relationship between drugs and violence. The second article highlights this aspect of the drug trade, while the third presents a sobering picture of the economic and political influences that enhance continued international production of illicit substances, in this case in Afghanistan. Is better treatment the option? Abstinence-only approaches do not appear particularly effective. The fourth article discusses some of the pharmaceutical and treatment perspectives that may provide hope for better alternatives.

As you read the following articles, consider how you would answer these questions.

38. Cocaine Prices Rise and Quality Declines, White House Says (11/18/05)

- To what did the White House Office of National Drug Control Policy attribute the rise in cocaine prices?
- Where does most of the cocaine come from that is sold in the U.S.?

39. Rival Drug Gangs Turn the Streets of Nuevo Laredo into a War Zone (12/04/05)

- Why are the land routes for drug trafficking through Mexico so important?
- Why has the violence escalated in the last three years?

40. Da Bolan Dasht Journal: Another Year of Drug War, and the Poppy Crop Flourishes (02/17/06)

- How large is the increase in poppy cultivation in Afghanistan this year?
- What are the economic and political reasons the farmers grow poppy?

41. Ideas & Trends: Between Addiction and Abstinence (05/07/06)

- What is the "moderate use" idea in addiction treatment?
- How is moderate use related to pharmaceutical treatments for addiction?

Cocaine Prices Rise and Quality Declines, White House Says

By Juan Forero
November 18, 2005
(Correction Appended)

After years of disappointing news about the easy availability of cocaine on American streets, the Bush administration on Thursday said its multibillion-dollar drug war in Colombia was showing signs of success, with the retail price of the drug in the United States sharply higher and the level of purity lower.

From February to September, the price of a gram of cocaine rose 19 percent, to $170, while the purity level fell 15 percent, the White House Office of National Drug Control Policy said.

White House officials said those trends were consistent with a shortage of cocaine and validated the United States' $4 billion, multiyear plan to wipe out cocaine drug crops in Colombia through aerial spraying.

"These numbers confirm that the levels of interdiction, the levels of eradication, have reduced the availability of cocaine in the United States," John Walters, director of the White House Office of National Drug Control Policy, said Thursday in a telephone interview from Washington. "There's a change in availability. The policy is working."

But drug policy analysts critical of the administration's war on drugs said the White House was drawing unrealistically rosy conclusions from too short a period. They noted that a Rand Corporation study for the White House in 2003 showed that as the war on drugs had expanded since 1981, the price of cocaine had tumbled to historic lows while purity levels had risen.

Drug policy analysts also said that like any commodity, the price of cocaine sometimes fluctuates wildly. Yet the cocaine trade remains intractably lucrative, they said.

"Cocaine is not like computer chips, where new technology makes it cheaper and cheaper," said Ethan Nadelmann, executive director of the Lindesmith Center-Drug Policy Foundation, an independent New York group that says the war on drugs has been counterproductive. "A small blip upward after so many years of decline in price and increase in purity is essentially meaningless."

Since 2000, American officials have insisted that an aggressive push to spray land used for Colombia's huge drug crops with glyphosate would pay off. Hundreds of thousands of acres, many in a swath of southern Colombia held by Marxist rebels, have been sprayed.

But this year, even after reporting that 336,000 acres of coca plants had been sprayed in 2004, the White House

The overall picture is positive: seizures of cocaine are way up and cocaine use among some sectors of the American population has declined.

acknowledged that the amount of coca across Colombia was "statistically unchanged" from 2003.

Coca cultivation has spread to most states, growers are planting more potent strains and the amount of cocaine Colombia produces is still more than enough to satisfy American demand.

Right-wing paramilitary commanders have continued trafficking much of Colombia's cocaine, fearing little from the administration of President Álvaro Uribe, which has granted generous concessions shielding them from serious punishment as they participate in a government-sponsored disarmament process. Human rights groups and some Colombian political leaders say that the paramilitaries are evolving into a Mafia-like organization that depends on the cocaine trade.

John Walsh, who follows American drug policy for the Washington Office on Latin America, a policy analysis group, said cocaine trafficking regularly rebounded after difficult periods. When Colombia dismantled the Medellín cocaine cartel in the late 1980's and began an offensive against the Cali cartel in the mid-1990's, "cocaine price increases, while obvious, were equally obviously short-lived," he said. "They were quite ephemeral."

Still, the American government says the overall picture is positive: its figures show that seizures of cocaine are way up and that cocaine use among some sectors of the American population has declined.

The White House said the newest figures were just the start of a positive trend. Officials say that trend took time to develop because the traffickers had probably overproduced when the spraying effort began and for months used stockpiles of cocaine to supply American consumers.

"We kept watching this and watching this and that started to change,"

David Murray, a drug policy analyst at the White House, said of the price and purity figures. "Nobody is saying victory. We're just finding a figure that's consistent with some of the other data sets we had."

■ **Correction:** November 19, 2005, Saturday. An article yesterday about a Bush administration report on the price of cocaine misstated the name of an independent group whose director was quoted assessing the report. It is the Drug Policy Alliance and is no longer called the Lindesmith Center-Drug Policy Foundation.

Rival Drug Gangs Turn the Streets of Nuevo Laredo into a War Zone

By Ginger Thompson
December 4, 2005

The lucrative drug trade on the Mexican border seemed up for grabs after Mexican authorities arrested the powerful leader of the Gulf Cartel nearly three years ago. The rival Sinaloa Cartel sent Edgar Valdéz Villarreal, a young upstart known as La Barbie, to do the grabbing.

The wave of killings that followed has turned into an all-out drug war that has spread to almost every corner of Mexico, leaving about 1,000 people dead since March 2003 and bringing harsh criticisms from Washington about the failure of President Vicente Fox's government to end it.

The most spectacular gunfights began here last spring, federal law enforcement authorities said, and usually took place from 8 in the morning to 1 in the afternoon, on the elegant Avenida Colón.

While the number of killings has gone down since President Fox sent a battalion of federal officers to try to take back control of the city's streets, the violence has not ended but moved to other parts of Mexico, especially the central state of Michoacan and the Pacific coast resort of Acapulco.

The rise of men like Mr. Valdéz, 32, Deputy Attorney General José Santiago Vasconcelos said in an interview, helps explain why. He is part of a younger generation of rash and ruthless traffickers, Mr. Vasconcelos said, who are fighting to take over the drug trade after the Fox administration put at least a dozen of the older drug bosses in jail.

[Last week, law enforcement authorities linked Mr. Valdéz to a video that appeared to show the interrogation of four bruised and bloody men who admitted to being hired killers for the Gulf Cartel. The video, which was sent in an unmarked envelope to The Kitsap Sun in Washington State and was posted on the Web site of The Dallas Morning News, ended by showing one of the men being shot in the head. The authorities said they suspected that Mr. Valdéz was conducting the interrogation.]

The prize is the lucrative land drug routes that carry more than 77 percent of all the cocaine and about 70 percent of all the methamphetamines sold in the United States.

The more experienced drug kingpins, Mexican prosecutors said, were more willing to reach peace among themselves, to respect one another's territories and to stay out of sight in order not to cause trouble for local authorities.

New operatives like Mr. Valdéz, however, fight for all or nothing, Mr. Vasconcelos said. And they seem willing to keep up their fight, no matter what the cost.

"Why are we in this situation?" Mr. Vasconcelos said. "Because the only leaders who can contain the violence are the ones who are in jail."

"The structures they used to maintain—of corruption and obstruction of justice—when we took those away, they were forced to use violence," he said. "It's a beast."

Mr. Valdéz, a k a La Barbie, does not look like a monster. He gets his nickname, the authorities said, because he has the light complexion and blue eyes of a Ken doll. Law enforcement authorities, however, have described him as the mastermind of numerous killings and kidnappings across the country. They have raided homes that they believe had been rented by him and found grenades, automatic weapons and police uniforms.

Mr. Valdéz' illegal career took off after the arrest in March 2003 of Osiel Cárdenas, who controlled the drug trade in Nuevo Laredo, the busiest port along the 2,000-mile border between the United States and Mexico. Then his rival, Joaquín Guzmán, known as El Chapo, decided to make a move for control of this area.

Mr. Guzmán could not do it on his own, though. He had escaped from prison in 2001, and immediately became one of this country's most wanted fugitives. So while he hid in the mountains of Sinaloa state, the authorities said, he gave Mr. Valdéz, who is originally from Laredo, Tex., command of a well-trained unit of gunmen to lead the assault against the Gulf Cartel across the Rio Grande in Nuevo Laredo.

Mr. Valdéz and another lieutenant, Arturo Beltrán Leyva, went to Mexico City in March 2003 with a $1.5-million bribe for Domíngo Gonzalez Díaz, a commander in the Federal Investigations Agency, Mexico's F.B.I., Mexican authorities said. In exchange for the money, the authorities said, Mr. Gonzalez sent a close confidant to command federal forces here, with instructions to provide protection to the Sinaloa Cartel and to help it fight its rivals.

Two months later, that federal commander, Adolfo Ruiz Ibarra, was shot with his brother Edmundo in a blaze of gunfire. It was one of the first clear signs, the authorities said, that the Gulf Cartel would not surrender easily.

officers, known as Los Zetas, who had deserted from the military and served as Mr. Cárdenas's personal security detail when he was out of prison, were deployed to protect the Gulf Cartel's turf—especially Nuevo Laredo.

Mexican authorities say they believe Mr. Cárdenas was behind the killing in December 2004 of El Chapo's brother, who was also being held in La Palma. After that, authorities said, the fight between the Gulf Cartel and the Sinaloa Cartel turned personal.

Kidnapping and revenge killings became common. The Zetas would leave scathing notes near the bodies of their victims, and it was through such a note that mentioned Mr. Valdéz by name

But since then, his name has appeared on most-wanted lists from the United States Drug Enforcement Agency, which issued a warrant for his arrest in 2003 on charges of cocaine smuggling, and by the federal authorities in Mexico.

Rafael Ríos, the deputy secretary for public security, described Mr. Valdéz as "an operator in charge of distribution of drugs and of recruiting" new soldiers for the cartel. Most of the recruits come, as he did, from north of the border, and have helped expand the Sinaloa Cartel's operations, and its violence, into the United States.

In September 2004, Mr. Valdéz bought an entire page in El Norte, a daily newspaper here, to declare his innocence and ask President Fox for justice. He described himself as a legitimate businessman who had been forced to leave Nuevo Laredo and move to the neighboring state of Coahuila because he was being harassed for bribes from local police officers.

New operatives like Mr. Valdéz, however, fight for all or nothing. And they seem willing to keep up their fight, no matter what the cost.

Mr. Cárdenas, the leader of the Gulf Cartel, managed to keep control of his gang from inside Mexico's main maximum-security prison, La Palma. The Nuevo Laredo police department served almost entirely at his pleasure, federal law authorities said, helping not only protect the Gulf Cartel, but also kidnapping and killing suspected rivals. And a group of special forces

that the authorities learned he had crossed the border into Nuevo Laredo.

He did not have much of a criminal record before he left Texas, according to the Laredo police—just a reputation as a small-time drug dealer and a drunken driving charge nine years ago. "As far as we're concerned," said Juan Rivera, a spokesman for the Laredo Police Department, "he's nobody here."

"I ask you to intervene to resolve the insecurity, extortion and terror that exists in the state of Tamaulipas, and especially in the city of Nuevo Laredo," the letter read. In a later paid advertisement in the newspaper El Mañana, Mr. Valdéz asked the question on many Mexicans' minds: "Could it be that the Mexican Army and the attorney general lack the means and tools to finish these delinquents?"

Da Bolan Dasht Journal: Another Year of Drug War, and the Poppy Crop Flourishes

By Carlotta Gall
February 17, 2006

Already the green shoots of poppy plants are showing in the fields of Helmand, the top opium producing province in Afghanistan, and this year everyone—government officials, farm-

ers and aid workers alike—says there will be another bumper crop.

"Last year 40 percent of land was used for poppy cultivation," said Fazel Ahmad Sherzad, head of the anti-narcotics

department in Helmand. "This year it is up to 80 percent in places."

"Three months ago I came and told these farmers not to grow poppy, but look, it's all poppy," he added, gesturing at the bright green crop now showing across the acres between the mud-walled farmhouses.

The farmers in this village just 20 minutes' drive from the provincial capital, Lashkar Gah, did not seem the least bit embarrassed to be caught growing the illegal crop, which is processed into opium and heroin. One old farmer, Hajji Habibullah, even weeded his poppy crop while chatting with the anti-drug chief. "We have to grow it," he said. "We need the money."

Another farmer, Ahmad Jan, 62, agreed. He has planted 8 of his 10 acres with poppy. "We will not abandon

The farmers in this village say they have little choice. They live on land reclaimed from the desert. Nothing grows in the salty earth except the hardy poppy plant. They have to pump water for irrigation from a well nearly 100 yards deep, they say, and only high-priced opium makes the effort cost-effective. They would lose money if they tried to grow wheat or melons, they said.

"If they destroy the poppy we will have to leave the country," said another farmer, Pahlawan, 24, who uses only one name. "What else can we do in the desert?"

Asia Development Group, which helps farmers develop alternative crops. "This is the rebound effect."

Two farmers from the Nawa district south of Lashkar Gah, where the police did destroy the poppy crop last year, said that this year the farmers were hedging in every way they could. Some are growing double the usual amount of poppy because they are calculating that half of the crop may be eradicated. Others are growing smaller amounts behind walled gardens to see if they can get away with it, said one of the farmers, Jamal Khan, 24.

The Taliban, too, are promoting the growing, as a source of income for their operations. They have spread leaflets ordering farmers to grow poppy.

In Helmand, the Taliban have forged an alliance with drug smugglers, providing protection for drug convoys and mounting attacks to keep the government away and the poppy flourishing, the new governor of Helmand, Muhammad Daud, said.

Virtually all of the heroin sold in Russia and 75 percent of that sold in Europe originates in Afghanistan.

poppy cultivation until the end of this world," he said. "If the government does not give us anything first, we will not stop."

The Afghan government and its international backers are suffering from a serious lack of credibility when it comes to curbing poppy cultivation here. Despite the strictures of the government and the police, and personal pleas from President Hamid Karzai for farmers not to grow it, they have carried on anyway.

Poppy growing is so uncontrolled that despite millions of aid dollars spent to train anti-drug forces and to help farmers grow other crops, Afghanistan is showing no sign of leaving its position as the world's biggest producer of opium. It accounts for almost three-quarters of global opium production.

Virtually all of the heroin sold in Russia and 75 percent of that sold in Europe originates in Afghanistan, according to the United Nations Office on Drugs and Crime. Helmand Province, in Afghanistan's southwest, alone produces 40 percent of the country's poppy harvest.

But the farmers seem fairly confident that will not happen. "Even now they think the government will not destroy the poppy," Mr. Sherzad, the anti-drug chief, said of the farmers. "We even took people to Kabul for meetings to tell them, but still they think we will not cut it down."

Not without reason. Eradication last year was something of a joke, nearly all agree. The police brought in tractors to plow up the poppy fields, but much of it grew back and the farmers still managed to harvest a crop, Mr. Sherzad said.

The police can also be bribed to leave part of the crop, said the villagers, out of the hearing of the police. "We have money, so we are not scared," Mr. Pahlawan said.

They watched the neighboring provinces of Kandahar and Farah get away with increased cultivation last year, and even clashes with the eradication force from Kabul, trained by the United States contractor DynCorp, without repercussions.

"In Kandahar last year there was no pressure to stop growing poppy," said Steve Shaulis, who runs the Central

The threat of Taliban reprisals may be just another convenient excuse farmers have thought up, said Col. Muhammad Ayub, the deputy police chief of the province.

But there is little doubt that the Taliban and the drug smugglers have a strong influence in the villages. One agricultural worker employed on a program to develop alternative crops said he continued to grow poppy on some of his land, otherwise the other villagers would accuse him of working for the government.

The one bright spot is the work of agricultural aid organizations, which are quietly persuading farmers to plant fruit trees and vineyards on some of their land, drawing at least a percentage of cultivated land away from poppy and providing work in rural areas to ease widespread dependency on opium as the main cash earner.

But those efforts alone will not change things, said Muhammad Sardar, who runs a rural recovery program for Mercy Corps. "It is government policy and more local government involvement that is needed," he said.

Ideas & Trends: Between Addiction and Abstinence

By Benedict Carey
May 7, 2006

A humiliating accident. An apparent memory lapse. A sudden, emotional confession.

Representative Patrick Kennedy's car crash on Capitol Hill early Thursday and a news conference a day later had a familiar rhythm, especially for those who study addiction or know it firsthand.

Mr. Kennedy, a six-term Democrat from Rhode Island, said that his addiction was to prescription medication and that he planned to seek treatment at an addiction clinic, as he had done before.

"I struggle every day with this disease, as do millions of Americans," said Mr. Kennedy, who is 38.

But will a cure that apparently didn't take the first time be successful the second time around? Mr. Kennedy, for one, ruefully acknowledged how easy it was for him to backslide.

Mr. Kennedy is seeking treatment at a time when the entire field is undergoing a transformation. Once akin to exorcists, committed to casting out the demons altogether, those who work with addictive behavior of all kinds are

heavy, chronic drinkers in the study. Some quit altogether; most, however, had moderated their drinking—to 14 drinks a week or fewer for men, 11 or fewer for women.

"The fact is that these moderate measures are becoming more and more accepted in judging treatments," said Dr. Edward Nunes, a professor of clinical psychiatry at Columbia University.

Millions of recovering addicts and their families as well as counselors working in the trenches consider this approach to be foolhardy and immoral. Addicts are by definition unable to control or manage their addictions, they say, and leaving an opening for moderate use only encourages the experimentation that can lead to ruin or death.

Cases like that of Mr. Kennedy dramatically illustrate how close to breakdown many addicts live, they say. "Implying you can simply cut down does a tremendous disservice to those who have this addiction," said Stanley L., a recovering alcoholic in Pennsylvania who still attends group counseling sessions.

bling binges, is more likely to reduce the consumption than shut it down altogether. And perhaps the biggest recent advance in smoking cessation, the nicotine patch, is itself a badge of compromise, an admission that many smokers need a habit to lean on, temporarily or perhaps indefinitely, as they strive for life without.

When studying these pharmaceutical crutches and prescribing them, doctors tend to emphasize improvement over abstinence for good reasons, researchers say.

"Third-party payers," said Dr. Barbara Mason of the Scripps Research Institute, where she treats and studies addiction. "One way you can convince people holding the purse strings to cover treatment is to say, look, if you pay for this and it lowers the level of drinking or substance use you won't have to pay for E.R. visits. That's really important. If you prevent one case of fetal alcohol syndrome, you don't have to pay for a lifetime of care."

Some studies of drug use and gambling have also contributed to shifting the thinking about addiction. For example, surveys find that most smokers who quit do so on their own, after many attempts and periods of moderation. An estimated 20 percent of compulsive drug users and drinkers have had similar recoveries, experts say.

In a 2002 study, researchers at Harvard Medical School tracked the behavior of more than 6,000 casino employees, many of whom were heavy drinkers, gamblers or both. Over a period of three years, many of those with diagnosable disorders changed their behavior, moving from heavy use to moderate levels, and sometimes back up again.

"The conventional wisdom is that you get the habit and start down this

Offering moderate use as a first step, some therapists say, is the only way of "meeting people where they are."

now trying less dogmatic approaches—ones that allow for moderate use as a bridge to abstinence.

A government-financed study of alcoholism released last week, the largest to date, suggests how deeply this "moderate use" idea has taken hold. The study found that the treatment produced "good clinical outcomes" in about three-quarters of the almost 1,400

Yet the openness to moderate use is likely to increase, driven by changes in the science of addiction, like pharmaceutical treatments.

The latest option for opiate addiction, bupenorphine, is a substitute drug, like methadone, replacing one habit with another. The drug naltrexone, which seems to numb the brain to the euphoria from drinking or gam-

slippery slope and it just gets worse and worse, but that was not true for many of these people," said Christine Reilly, executive director of the Institute for Research on Pathological Gambling and Related Disorders, in Medford, Mass.

Heavy gamblers and drug users are much more diverse groups, in short, than many presume, and their compulsions have different meanings in the context of their lives that are important guides for treatment.

Some addicts are depressed and anxious and in need of psychotherapy but can't get it because therapists require that they give up their habits first, said Alan Marlatt, director of the Addictive Behaviors Research Center at the University of Washington. "Maybe the drug use is responsible for the depression, or the depression led to the drug, but it's all mixed up and they never find out, because they can't get treatment," he said.

Many addicts, it is true, spiral only downward, and must quit to stay alive. But others are ambivalent about whether they want to quit or not. Their routines, their pleasures, some of their most sustaining relationships are tied up with their habits, and it is far from clear what will nourish them if they suddenly give up. The very idea, common in abstinence-based programs, that one "slip" can lead to total loss of control may undermine their best efforts to self-regulate.

"It's very scary for them to contemplate life without this habit, because it has become very meaningful for them," Ms. Reilly said.

Offering moderate use as a first step, some therapists say, is the only way of "meeting people where they are," and getting them down to a level of use that keeps them from driving under the influence, petty crime or other trouble.

"The idea is to reduce the consequences of the heavy use, and work from there," said Mr. Marlatt.

This was more or less the view offered by Charles Barkley, the former N.B.A. star, in an interview on ESPN last week:

"Do I have a gambling problem? Yeah, I do have a gambling problem but I don't consider it a problem because I can afford to gamble. It's just a stupid habit that I've got to get under control, because it's just not a good thing to be broke after all of these years."

By treating the habit as just that—a habit—and not a disease, therapists may be able to make progress in reducing the bad consequences, whether a broken marriage or an embarrassing car accident.

On the other hand, the risk to addicts of this approach is incontestably real, and no one knows in advance who can and cannot safely moderate their addictive behavior.

"I am deeply concerned about my reaction to the medication and my lack of knowledge of the accident that evening," Representative Kennedy said on Friday. "But I do know enough to know that I need to seek expert help."

XI. PERSPECTIVES ON CHILD WELFARE

As can be seen in the four articles dealing with child welfare, the child welfare system can be described as a national crisis. In each case, reform efforts to improve the delivery of child welfare services have been substantially assisted by federal court mandates. The first article describes the significant improvement in Alabama that resulted from court-mandated changes. In the second, the failure of New Jersey to effectively implement changes negotiated in federal court demonstrate the difficulty of affecting meaningful change in a timely basis. In order to pay for state welfare agencies, the Social Security benefits provided to the children are seized by the states. The third article questions the appropriateness of this funding transfer by asking if it is really in the interests of the children. In order to increase the adoption of foster children, adoptive parents may qualify for financial subsidies. The fourth article discusses one attempt to eliminate this subsidy and how this change is likely to result in increased state costs for foster care.

As you read the following articles, consider how you would answer these questions.

42. Once Woeful, Alabama Is Model in Child Welfare (08/20/05)

- How much did case loads drop?
- How much did the reform of child welfare in Alabama cost?

43. New Jersey Child Welfare System Is Missing Its Own Targets (12/16/05)

- How effective has New Jersey's regular medical visit policy been in examining children removed from their homes?
- What are the barriers to effective implementation of the Comprehensive Health Evaluations for Children?

44. Welfare Agencies Seek Foster Children's Assets (02/17/06)

- How much money are state welfare agencies taking from the Social Security benefits provided to foster children?
- When does a foster child's Supplemental Security Income end?

45. Judge Bars Subsidy Cuts in Adopting Foster Children (05/02/06)

- Why did Judge Wright issue a permanent injunction against cutting aid to parents adopting foster children?
- How much is distributed to adoptive parents in aid annually?

Once Woeful, Alabama Is Model in Child Welfare

By Erik Eckholm
August 20, 2005

As a mother, Stephanie Harris seemed hopeless. She was 29 and a determined crack addict back in 1993, when she was sent to prison for neglecting her six children, including infant twins. The authorities had little choice, she now agrees, but to give custody of her children to relatives.

"It didn't bother me," she recalled in a recent interview. "All I wanted to do was get high."

She served eight months, failed a urine test and went back to prison for a year.

If history were the guide, in Alabama or perhaps any other state, Ms. Harris might never have regained her children, child welfare officials here say. More likely, the children would have been shuffled among relatives and foster homes.

But officials here had, under court supervision, begun a wholesale overhaul of the child protection system to make it more pro-family, and they did not give up on Ms. Harris. Today she is off drugs, has a job and has custody of all but one of her children, whom an aunt is fighting to keep.

Her case illustrates what experts in child welfare say has been one of the country's most sweeping transformations of the handling of neglected and abused children. What by all accounts had been a dysfunctional system in Alabama, scarring too many children by sending them to foster-care oblivion while ignoring others in danger, has over the last 14 years become a widely studied model. But it has not been cheap, and in some ways Alabama has had to be dragged onto its pedestal because of political and philosophical resistance to the reforms and in spite of the state's endemic poverty.

"Alabama set the pace," said Richard Wexler, director of the National Coali-

tion for Child Protection Reform, a private group in Alexandria, Va. "Though they've had some setbacks, I still view Alabama as a national model."

Forced by a legal settlement to make changes after parents and advocates filed a class-action lawsuit charging that the system failed to aid troubled families or protect children from neglect or abuse, Alabama has more than quadrupled its spending on child welfare since 1990, even as it has trimmed other programs in recent years.

One former governor, Fob James, complained about federal interference and questioned whether so much devotion to helping irresponsible parents was leaving children in harm's way. While Mr. James's successors have accepted the changes, they still resent being monitored; in a court brief this month, Attorney General Troy King said that the continuing court supervision defied the principle of "democratic self-rule through officials answerable to the people."

While Alabama's system is far from perfect, local officials and independent experts say, the system now is more likely than before to keep children with their parents, safely, and tries to provide whatever aid might help that happen.

Typical caseloads for social workers have been trimmed to 18 from 50, allowing far more intensive monitoring of families and help. Where reports of neglect or abuse sometimes lay unchecked for months, investigators are now usually on the scene within a day when danger is imminent, and within five days more than 90 percent of the time, officials report.

In what many call the best measure of a system's ability to protect children from abuse—the share of children who are mistreated after intervention by social workers—Alabama has steadily

improved its record. In recent years, a second abuse incident within 12 months of the first one occurred in roughly 5 percent of cases, down from about 13 percent in the early 1990's. Studies indicate that the comparable national average is about 11 percent.

And in a recent federal survey of child welfare systems, Alabama was one of only six states found to be "substantially in compliance" with norms for protecting children from neglect or abuse.

"When the lawsuit was filed, we didn't have the services that could keep children at home safely," said Carolyn B. Lapsley, the state's deputy commissioner for children and family services and a veteran social worker. "Now we're very proud; we have changed the system in every single county."

Though Alabama says it has made enough progress that it should be released from court supervision, skeptics question whether the new, labor-intensive practices can be maintained in the face of stringent budgets, high poverty and other social ills, including methamphetamine use, which state officials blame for a recent rise in the number of children removed from homes.

"We do not dispute that the agency has made progress," said James Tucker, a children's advocate and a lawyer in the suit that produced court monitoring.

"However, we believe that their recent efforts have focused more on creating a paper trail that looks like reform than producing the real reforms we seek," Mr. Tucker said, adding that some counties were lagging substantially, for example, in provision of vital family services.

Judge Ira DeMent of Federal District Court in Montgomery ruled in May that the state had not proved it could sustain its gains and declined to end the oversight for now. The state has asked him to reconsider.

When the class-action suit was filed, in 1988, "those who looked at the Alabama system invariably judged it as one of the worst in the country," Mr. Tucker said.

The 1991 settlement committed the state to a series of principles: quick investigations to head off danger, family preservation if possible, wide-ranging services for struggling parents and faster adoption for those requiring it, among others.

Ira Burnim, a lawyer with the Bazelon Center for Mental Health Law in Washington who helped draw up the agreement, said parents were often seen more as threats than as potential partners. And, Mr. Burnim said, "there's a traditional tendency to focus on 'saving' the children but also to see them as damaged goods."

Child-welfare spending that totaled $71 million in 1990, including $47 million in federal money, rose to $285 million in 2004, $179 million of it from the federal government. Some of that came from Medicaid money the state had not previously tapped.

The state hired hundreds of new social workers and thinned caseloads. Workers could now spend more than 10 hours a week in some homes.

Cindy Letson, who lives in the small town of Moulton in the corn and poultry country of northern Alabama, has seen firsthand how the system works.

Her face weathered beyond her 48 years, Ms. Letson described a history of family violence and recalled the day in 2001 when the police took her for psychiatric evaluation.

She returned home within a day cleared of any serious disorder, she said, but was sent for counseling and help in breaking an addiction to antiseizure drugs. Her twin boys had already been removed and were sent to foster parents.

She followed the directives and was allowed to visit her boys for one hour

a week. After repeated entreaties she regained custody two years ago, and now lives on welfare with her 7-year-old boys, Kyle and Kenley.

"I was ready to give up, but in the end the system worked," Ms. Letson said.

Elements of Alabama's approach have been adopted by other states. "A

lot of the ideas we used came from the Alabama example," said Benjamin Wolf of the Illinois A.C.L.U., who has helped design changes to the system in Illinois, which is also operating under court supervision.

Alabama's method of evaluating its own system — choosing individual cases and closely examining how each was handled — has been adopted by the federal government for its assessment of child-welfare systems in each state, said Olivia A. Golden, a former federal welfare official now with the Urban Institute in Washington. New York City has also adopted the method.

But here, as in every state, there remain lapses. [On Wednesday, a state judge criticized the Jefferson County Department of Human Resources for failing to protect 2-year-old Sean Porter, who suffered severe bruising to his groin last December, two weeks after school officials reported suspicious bruises on his sister, the Birmingham News reported.]

In a report last November, Ivor D. Groves, a welfare expert from Florida who is Alabama's court-appointed monitor, said the state's progress toward the original reform goals had varied by county.

But without question, Mr. Groves said, "the egregious conditions of impossible caseloads and large numbers of uninvestigated" abuse and neglect reports "have been eliminated."

Some Alabama counties show "the best child-welfare practice in the country," Mr. Groves wrote.

The share of children who are mistreated after intervention by social workers [is down to] 5 percent. Studies indicate that the comparable national average is about 11 percent.

Ms. Harris, in Montgomery, has been a beneficiary of Alabama's progress. As she emerged from work-release and a third drug-treatment program in 1995, she showed that she was serious about going straight. So caseworkers, while requiring regular drug tests, helped Ms. Harris rebuild her life and then regain her children.

They paid for years of counseling and helped with expenses like child care, utility bills and, at one point, Christmas presents and shoes for the children.

Ms. Harris has since borne two more children and lives in a subsidized redbrick house in Montgomery with five of her children.

She works the day shift as a carhop and scrambles to provide for her boisterous clan, supplementing her income with Social Security payments for a child needing special education and a father's child support for two of them.

"My social worker was there for me," she said. "I've learned to pay my bills and manage my life."

In June, the child agency finally closed its books on Ms. Harris, satisfied that she could provide a decent home.

New Jersey Child Welfare System Is Missing Its Own Targets

By Tina Kelley and Richard Lezin Jones
December 16, 2005

Two years ago, New Jersey's child welfare system began a wrenching self-examination after the discovery of four emaciated children, the Jackson brothers, who the authorities said had been systematically starved by their adoptive parents.

When officials asked how such neglect could have been prevented, one suggestion seemed simple: regular medical visits. The state made prompt checkups for children entering foster care a cornerstone of its court-ordered overhaul, requiring that children who were removed from their homes have a comprehensive medical examination within 30 days.

But more than 18 months into the state's child welfare reform effort, and more than a year after these exams were required, New Jersey officials are failing to provide those medical checks to about 80 percent of eligible children, despite spending hundreds of thousands of dollars in additional state money for health care.

The difficulties that New Jersey has had in providing the promised medical exams offer a glimpse into some of the obstacles that the state has faced in trying to repair its child welfare system.

State and medical officials said that staff shortages, a delay in financing and poor communication between caseworkers and foster parents had hampered the state's efforts to offer the exams. Fewer clinics than expected volunteered to give the time-consuming and expensive exams. In part, that was because additional state money was not initially offered to them, and in part because medical experts in child abuse are scarce.

At some of the seven clinics around the state conducting the exams, doctors say that the state has sent them a fraction of the patients they could see; others complain that they are overburdened and weeks behind schedule in conducting the checkups.

One clinic complained of a cancellation rate as high as 50 percent because of confusion among foster families and caseworkers about appointments. And doctors say that caseworkers still do not receive consistent training about the need for the exams, with some never having heard of them.

As a result, hundreds of children who should be evaluated under the state's new medical standard are not being seen. A study by the state's child advocate, to be released in the next few days, found that of the approximately 5,500 children placed in foster care by the state this year, fewer than 20 percent received the medical and mental health assessments called for in the reform plan.

Almost two out of three of the medical problems discovered in exams did not get follow-up treatment, according to one sampling, including diagnoses of psychiatric problems, asthma, anemia and speech delays. Kevin M. Ryan, the state's child advocate, said the state's slow response might be putting children at risk.

"The starvation and medical neglect of the Jackson boys should have put to rest any doubt that we need to build a statewide health care system for foster children," he said. "We uncovered their plight more than two years ago, so the time lag is incredibly frustrating."

New Jersey has committed more than $320 million during the past two years to improve its child welfare system, following a plan state officials helped create to settle a class-action lawsuit filed by Children's Rights Inc., an advocacy group based in Manhattan.

Yet lawyers representing foster children in the suit found that so little progress had been made that they filed a request with a federal judge this month calling for an emergency takeover of the system and for Jon S. Corzine, the governor-elect, to be put in charge of fixing it.

The state defends how it has spent its money, but says that the timetable—one that the state had agreed to—has been too ambitious. The panel monitoring the state's progress in the overhaul has said it would be willing to adjust the deadline for meeting the new medical standards if the state demonstrated sufficient progress in meeting them or offered a reasonable explanation for why a delay was necessary.

To be sure, the state has made improvements in the past two years, hiring more than 1,000 new caseworkers and removing more than 100 mentally ill children from juvenile detention centers, where they had been illegally held because the state had nowhere else to put them.

But the state has spent all the money allocated for some improvements, such as more visits by caseworkers, while failing to make the targeted number of visits. It has also struggled with starting up a staff training academy and introducing a computer system to help better track children; the computer system, first scheduled for completion in March 2006, is now expected to be in use by November 2007.

However, of the state's shortcomings, its failure to put comprehensive medical checkups in place is among the most potentially dangerous, officials say.

"Nothing is more fundamental to kids' well-being than their getting good health care," said Steve Cohen, a member of the monitoring panel. "We see the state is really unable to assure good medical care for kids for whom it has taken custody."

The state, under its court-ordered reform plan, agreed that as of Dec. 31, 98 percent of children would get the new medical exams within the first month of entering foster care.

Fewer than 20 percent received the medical and mental health assessments called for in the reform plan.

Last week, Human Services Commissioner James M. Davy testified before the New Jersey Assembly's budget committee that the system would miss that deadline.

He also conceded that there were serious concerns about putting the exams in place. "I'll be honest with you, we're having some problems with the way that it is working," Mr. Davy told lawmakers.

So far, state officials say, slightly fewer than 1,000 children have received the exam out of more than 5,500 who have been eligible since they began last year. Child welfare officials said that number is skewed slightly by children who are in the system for fewer than 30 days and not subject to the requirement, although they did not provide an estimate on how many children fit into that category.

Mr. Davy has offered no estimate of when the state might be able to meet the court-ordered standard. At the same time, there are no plans to expand the exams to include children already in the state's care.

The exams are the middle tier of the state's ambitious three-part plan to improve health care for children. Children who are removed from their homes receive a preplacement exam immediately. Then there is the more detailed new exam, called the Comprehensive Health Evaluations for Children, or CHEC. Finally, before children move within the system, for example from one foster home to another, they are required to get a third health screening.

But the exam program, which few other states have tried and which a

national advocate called commendable for including mental health issues, has struggled from its inception, in part because it was so ambitious. The exams last up to four hours and involve childhood mental health experts, who are scarce and notoriously overbooked.

"One could have thought of this as a pilot program," said Dr. Joseph J. Jacobs, the medical director for New Jersey's child welfare agency, the Division of Youth and Family Services. "We kind of jumped to a full-blown, statewide program."

Only seven sites agreed to provide the exams, which cost as much as $1,100; Medicaid reimburses them for only $670 of that.

While Dr. Jacobs said clinics had not complained about the amount of the reimbursement, he said, "the lack of additional funding to hire more staff up front may have been a barrier."

Once most of the clinics were running, the state agreed to give four of them an additional $130,000 to help cover costs. Now state officials plan to budget that amount for each of 15 clinics next year, with the goal of accommodating every eligible child, Dr. Jacobs said.

The state, however, had limited control over where the clinics were located.

The clinics that volunteered to do the exams were not all located close to the areas with the largest number of children entering foster care, causing some to be overbooked and others to be underused. The system also relies on the local child welfare office to refer children efficiently, which does not always happen.

One place that offers such exams, the New Jersey Child Abuse Research Education Service Institute, at the Stratford campus of the University of Medicine and Dentistry of New Jersey,

and serving a region that includes impoverished Camden, is falling far short of the 600 examinations it is prepared to conduct yearly. In anticipation of the demand, it took additional office space and hired a doctor, a nurse practitioner and several part-time psychologists, said its director, Martin A. Finkel.

By the end of October, the state had referred just 222 patients to the clinic, Dr. Finkel said.

He said that another clinic in Hackensack was prepared to provide a similar number of exams but had so far received only 179 patients.

At the same time, Dr. Jacobs said, some of the five other sites are "absolutely inundated with referrals." One of those is the Jersey Shore Medical Center in Neptune, where Dr. Steven W. Kairys said that there is about a two-month wait for exams.

Dr. Kairys, who supervises the CHEC program at the Neptune clinic, said that the center could use more staff members, although it recently used grant money to hire an extra nurse and a psychologist to help with the exams. The volume of cases that the center sees is so great, he said, that ideally two additional sites are needed.

Because of the backlog, Dr. Kairys said, his office has seen only about 140 of the 700 children in Monmouth and Ocean Counties who have entered the child welfare system since the center started performing the exams six months ago.

"These are some of the most vulnerable and most damaged children in the state," Dr. Kairys said. "So having them evaluated to catch up with them soon after they come into the state's eye is crucial."

Dr. Jacobs said that some children taken from homes in one county might have been placed with foster families in another county, which would skew calculations about how many exams needed to be done in each. The state has worked to find clinics to provide exams near where there are backlogs.

Compounding the problem, Dr. Kairys said, is poor communication between social workers and foster parents. The foster parents often take the children to the visits, although it is the state's responsibility to ensure that the exams take place. As a result, about half the time, appointments are canceled or the children simply fail to show up, he said.

Dr. Finkel said caseworkers are also not clear about the rules. Because of all the new employees, and the delays in training them, many new case-workers are young, inexperienced and overwhelmed.

"There are all these mandates for caseworkers, but they don't know which ones to do first," he said. "There are caseworkers who haven't even heard of the CHEC program."

Some of the clinics said they could use more help, but hiring doctors who are experts in child abuse issues can take up to a year, as there are fewer than 100 who do such work full time in the country, Dr. Finkel said.

Mr. Ryan, the child advocate, remained hopeful that the system of providing care to foster children can be fixed. "This is about keeping our kids safe," he said. "We need to bring the right people together and get this done."

Welfare Agencies Seek Foster Children's Assets

By Erik Eckholm
February 17, 2006

In 2004, at the age of 14 and at his own desperate request, John G. became a ward of North Carolina.

His mother abandoned him for crack when he was 3, and his adoptive father died of cancer a year later. A succession of guardians beat him, made him sell drugs and refused to buy him toys.

When he finally arrived at a county-financed group residence, he was wearing outgrown clothes. On the plus side, he was receiving Social Security survivor benefits and he held title to a modest house, willed to him by the adoptive father 10 years earlier and an asset that might give him traction, or at least a place to live, when he "ages out" of foster care at 18.

Now, the fate of the house—and the insistence of Guilford County officials on taking all of John's Social Security benefits to help pay for his foster care—are at the center of a legal battle with potential repercussions around the country.

The dispute is the latest in a continuing struggle between children's advocates and money-starved welfare agencies. They are wrestling over the proper use of more than $100 million in Social Security benefits that the states are taking on behalf of foster children with disabilities or a dead or disabled natural parent.

Determined to extract as much federal aid for social programs as the law will permit, some state welfare agencies even hire private companies, working for contingency fees, to help them reap more federal money by identifying foster children who are eligible for Social Security benefits. The money is then routinely used to help offset the cost of foster care.

Advocates for children question the wholesale takeover of money, accusing agencies of repaying themselves for care they are obligated to provide and of failing to use the windfall to meet children's individual needs, whether extra tutoring or counseling or, as in John's case, something more unusual.

Guilford County officials refused to release any of John's money, even when they learned that his last guardian had stopped making the $221 monthly mortgage payments on his house and that he faced its imminent loss. A local court has ordered the county to make payments for now, but the county has appealed and said it might appeal to the United States Supreme Court if necessary.

For John, who as a foster child may not be fully identified, it was clear as he visited the house recently that it represented not just money but also a precious link to his troubled past and an unknown future.

"This is my childhood," John, now 15, said as he climbed through a broken window to explore the boarded-up structure for the first time since he fled it two years ago. On the floor of the bedroom, he found a brown teddy bear and clung to it, saying softly, "My mother gave this to me before she left."

John has no idea how he will support himself, but he wants to live in the house he inherited, a property valued at $80,000. "It will be a good place to be," he said.

John's court-appointed volunteer protector found out about the threat to his house and enlisted a Legal Aid lawyer to help him fight for it.

"For the state to pocket a child's money and allow his home to go into foreclosure just doesn't make sense," said his Legal Aid lawyer, Lewis Pitts. "No one can say it's in the best interests of the child."

The benefits that states routinely take include both Supplemental Security Income, or S.S.I., and other Social Security money for children whose parents have died or are disabled. The payments are often close to $600 a month, and usually end when children reach 18 or 21.

"The practice is not the result of deliberative policy discussions regarding how to best serve children in foster care," said Daniel L. Hatcher, a law professor at the University of Baltimore who is the author of an article on the subject that is to be published in The Cardozo Law Review. "It is simply an ad hoc reaction by underfunded state agencies."

"The Social Security benefits are treated as a funding stream," Mr. Hatcher said, rather than as an opportunity to provide any special services or to give children savings for the perilous months after they turn 18, when many fall into crime or homelessness.

A Supreme Court decision in 2003, overturning a decision by courts in Washington State, affirmed that states could legally use children's Social Security benefits to offset current "maintenance costs." But it did not address a deeper question: does that always serve the child's "best interests," as federal rules require, or the longer-term interests of the public for that matter?

In the case of John G., a Guilford County district court ruled last Dec. 29 that the state must pay up the mortgage and cover repairs so the house could be saved for the youth. Reviewing John's rough history and uncertain prospects, Judge Susan E. Bray declared that "any reasonable person would see the fiscal wisdom" of helping him keep the property.

The county has appealed to a higher state court, arguing that the state courts have no jurisdiction over the matter, that the county is legally entitled to use John's benefits to cover his care and that it has no responsibility to exhaust public resources so a child can own property.

"The federal regulations say that the funds are to be used for current needs and expenses," said Lynne Shifton, an assistant county attorney. "His house payments are not, in our opinion, to meet his current needs."

For now, the county must pay up the arrears on John's house and for needed repairs. A private group hopes to rent it

as a transition home for foster children until John is able to move in.

State governments around the country stoutly defend their use of foster children's benefits.

Twenty-six states filed a supporting brief to the Supreme Court in the 2003 Washington case, noting that the practice had been approved by the Social Security Administration and arguing that barring it "could leave the states in a position of economic peril."

If states cannot devote money to current care, the brief added, children will ultimately suffer because the states will not help eligible children sign up for benefits.

Many advocates for children agree with that point: preserving an incentive to enroll more children is good for them because the benefits will continue if the child is adopted or returns to his birth family.

"If you tinker seriously with incentives of the child welfare agency, you can wind up doing a lot of harm," said Bruce Boyer, director of the child law clinic at Loyola University in Chicago.

Mr. Boyer led a lawsuit that stopped Illinois from using benefits to cover, in addition to direct care expenses, the overhead costs of foster agencies.

Mr. Boyer said state governments had an inherent conflict of interest, serving as creditors trying to recoup the cost of their programs and also as trustees of children's money. As a first step, he said, agencies should try harder to find relatives or volunteers to serve as official recipients of benefits.

A new law in California, passed with the support of advocates for children, requires counties to evaluate each foster child for Social Security eligibility. But it also demands new scrutiny of how benefits are used and modest savings to help aging-out children become independent.

State governments had an inherent conflict of interest, serving as creditors trying to recoup the cost of their programs and also as trustees of children's money.

"We are moving toward an individualized system, requiring counties to stop and think about the child at every stage of the process—in choosing a payee, determining how to spend the money, and accounting for how the funds are spent," said Angie Schwartz, a lawyer at the National Center for Youth Law in Oakland, Calif.

During John G.'s recent visit to his house, it became clear that the property may offer John more than shelter.

Its yard overgrown, its front plastered with a "condemned" poster because the utilities were cut off, the vacant house is an eyesore in a tidy cul-de-sac of similar homes, all built by Habitat for Humanity.

But neighbors poured forth with hugs and joy when John showed up unexpectedly and said that he hoped to move back.

"He's had it real tough, but he's a good kid," said a mother from across the street.

As he left to return to his foster home—he has recently moved from the group facility to a private home—John vowed that he would return to the house in a few weeks, to mow the lawn.

Judge Bars Subsidy Cuts in Adopting Foster Children

By Erik Eckholm
May 2, 2006

A federal judge in Missouri yesterday blocked a state law that cut aid to parents adopting foster children, ruling that it violated federal statutes and the Constitution's equal protection clause.

The case had been watched by children's advocates nationally, who said the law, which passed last year as part of a broader effort to curb social spending, was a dangerous precedent that would undercut the adoption prospects of troubled children.

"We hope that this decision will stem efforts around the country to find inventive ways to cut budgets while harming voiceless populations," said Ira P. Lustbader, a lawyer with Children's Rights, a group in New York that joined in the case with local advocates and parents' groups. "This law made no sense as a legal matter, as a policy matter or as an economic matter."

Gov. Matt Blunt, a Republican, had pushed the law, saying that adoption

The state said that such subsidies cost it $60 million a year and that the law would save it $12 million.

Critics said that by discouraging adoptions the law would end up costing the state more over time in foster expenses and in later social costs, because so many former foster children end up homeless, with drug problems or in prison.

Finding permanent homes for foster children who cannot return to their biological parents is a national goal, backed up by federal, state and local subsidies for adoptive parents who are often taking on children with cognitive or medical disabilities. In Missouri, such payments can range from $225 to $650 a month, depending on needs for therapy or other special care.

The law required adoptive parents to reapply for subsidies annually, voiding contracts that had guaranteed aid to age 18. For a subgroup of parents, whose children were not covered by a federal

because it applied just to a subgroup without rational justification.

"The means test will not save taxpayer money, but will increase the overall cost of child welfare in the State of Missouri," he said. Several states have acted to curb adoption subsidies or eligibility, but the Missouri law went further than others by retroactively imposing means tests and other changes on parents who had adopted in the past.

Promoting the adoption of foster children who cannot return to their biological parents was a goal of federal laws passed in 1980 and 1997. Such adoptions have increased to 50,000 in recent years from 28,000 in 1996.

Related aid to parents has grown, reaching $4 billion last year, with half paid by the federal government, according to a study in the March issue of The Social Service Review.

The increasing costs have drawn the scrutiny of financially beleaguered states.

If a subsidy cut discourages adoptions, that is likely to prove shortsighted, said Richard P. Barth, a professor of social welfare at the University of North Carolina. Professor Barth is a co-author of the March study, which found that the public cost of supporting a child in the foster system tended to surpass significantly any adoption subsidies.

The public cost of supporting a child in the foster system tended to surpass significantly any adoption subsidies.

subsidies were spiraling out of control and that it made sense to focus money on the neediest parents. The governor did not issue a statement yesterday.

Hours after the ruling, by Judge Scott O. Wright of United States District Court in St. Louis, the state filed a notice of appeal with the United States Court of Appeals for the Eighth Circuit, a spokesman for the state attorney general's office, John Fougere, said.

program that bars means tests, it ended aid if the parents earned more than 200 percent of the poverty line, or $38,314 a year for a family of four.

In August, Judge Wright temporarily delayed invoking the law. After a one-day trial last week, he issued a permanent injunction yesterday, saying that the annual renewal of subsidy agreements violated federal law and that the means test was discriminatory

"Our research shows that adoptive parents pay quite a substantial amount for services that their children need, and this is only partly offset by the subsidies they receive," Professor Barth said. "These parents are taking on a substantial challenge and deserve the appreciation of the public."

XII. PERSPECTIVES ON GLOBALIZATION AND GLOBAL COMPETITION

Foreign trade imbalances, export markets, and other international economic indices may appear as a new language in social welfare, but there is little doubt that globalization and the effects of global competition are having substantial influence on domestic welfare policy. The first article documents the continuing decline in America's manufacturing base, suggesting that the future of the economy lies in high-value services. Recent trends in business schools dealing with the new science of services, as described in the second article, support this argument. The birth-to-grave welfare state described in the third article provides one possible approach to providing the education and training infrastructure necessary to sustain movement from manufacturing to high-value services, but requires funding commitments far exceeding national norms. Of course, globalization does not only affect America as the discussion of the challenges facing Italy in the fourth article makes clear. One solution proposed for Italy is movement toward high-value services. Is the only solution to global competition a race to become the most educated elite? If so, how are the average man and woman going to compete?

As you read the following articles, consider how you would answer these questions.

46. Economic View: Exporting Expertise, If Not Much Else (01/22/06)

- How far have durable and nondurable goods manufacturing fallen in the U.S. economy?
- What is wrong with the national economy relying on high-value services and sophisticated manufacturing rather than exports?

47. Academia Dissects the Service Sector, but Is It a Science? (04/18/06)

- What is "services science?"
- What effect will services science have on low-wage service jobs?

48. Letter from Sweden: An Economy with Safety Features, Sort of Like a Volvo (05/10/06)

- How could the loss of Marie-Louise Nordstrom's 35 year job be described as "relatively painless?"
- What seems to be the crucial element in the "Nordic model?"

49. Italy's Once-Plucky Little Factories Now Complicate Its Battle with "Made in China" (05/14/06)

- Why are Italy's family-owned businesses less competitive internationally?
- What are some of the proposed solutions to Italy's problems?

Economic View: Exporting Expertise, If Not Much Else

By Daniel Altman
January 22, 2006

Want to understand what's really happening in the American economy? Wade into the sea of numbers that pour out of Washington's prolific statistical agencies. They describe some disturbing changes.

You can look at the economy in two ways: by production, or by people. The two aren't always the same, because the amount of stuff that a given worker can generate in a given industry changes over time. This is clear when you look carefully at the biggest long-term trend in the economy: the decline of manufacturing.

Both of manufacturing's two big categories, durable goods (like cars and cable TV boxes) and nondurable goods (like pastrami and pantyhose), have plunged, but the exact trends have differed.

From 1965 to 2005, the percentage of payroll employees devoted to durable goods dropped to 8 percent, from 19 percent; over the same period, the share of the economy they represent shrank by just four percentage points. In other words, workers in these industries became a lot more productive as their numbers dwindled.

The picture was different for nondurable goods. In that category, the employees' share of the nation's labor force also declined steeply, by nine percentage points, to just 5 percent of the total. But nondurables' share of the economy dropped by even more, by 10 percentage points. If there were productivity gains, they were small enough to be obscured by quality and price changes.

Most of the losses in nondurable production had already occurred by the early 1990's. That's not too surprising, when you think about it: the nation's agriculture had become about as efficient as it could be, and clothing imports from developing countries like China, Bangladesh and Mauritius were in full swing.

The story for durable goods is more troubling. Half of the decline in production has been a legacy of the last recession: sales went down, and they have stayed down.

The situation is a first, and it has been reflected in the labor market, too. After the four recessions that occurred between 1973 and 1991, payroll employment for the manufacturing of durable goods dropped to about 10 million. But after the 2001 recession, it sank below nine million and hasn't picked up.

Increases in productivity could account for some of the lost jobs. But in a recent working paper, William D. Nordhaus, a professor of economics at Yale, surmised that productivity improvements in manufacturing had not pulled down employment across the entire sector, because the gains stimulated overall demand by making finished goods cheaper.

The explanation may lie instead in the world's emerging economies. They saturated the American market with nondurables in the 1980's and early 90's, using the profits to move onto higher-value, durable items.

The change in the trend for durable goods was not the only worrisome legacy of the last recession. In the information sector, which had been among the most steadily growing areas of the labor market, growth has completely stalled after taking a dive in 2001 and 2002. The relatively small industries of broadcasting and Internet publishing have started upward again. But in print publishing, telecommunications and Internet services, the trend has been absolutely flat, despite the economy's return to regular growth.

Of course, there have been winners, too. The share of the economy devoted to medical care services has grown by eight percentage points in the past four decades, with commensurate changes in employment. But this isn't necessarily great news for the economy. With exceptions like online consultations and robotic surgery, medical care services are not as easy to export as, for example, medical equipment.

We are becoming a nation of advisers, fixers, entertainers and high-tech engineers, with a lucrative sideline in treating our own illnesses.

The leisure and recreational industries have also expanded, with the share of employment up by four percentage points. Here, too, exporting is difficult: after all, gambling, artistic performances and restaurant dinners usually take place on site.

More promising, management and professional services like law and finance resumed their strong growth after taking a hit in the recession. These areas are the ripest for exporting. Need some business advice? No problem. Want some derivatives structured? Great. First, however, we need to train those consultants and bankers.

In the past, the United States profitably exported products of all types, from basic textiles to the latest surgical machinery. Now, it seems, the economy is coming to rely more on the highest-value services and sophisticated manufacturing. We are becoming a nation of advisers, fixers, entertainers and high-tech engineers, with a lucrative sideline in treating our own illnesses.

The change is being forced on us by global competition and our own aptitudes. The first step in dealing with it is to realize what's happening. The second, most likely, is to prepare for more of the same.

Academia Dissects the Service Sector, but Is It a Science?

By Steve Lohr
April 18, 2006

On his Asian trip last month, President Bush urged Americans not to fear the rise toward prosperity of emerging economies like India. Education, Mr. Bush said, was the best response to globalization, climbing further up the ladder of skills to "fill the jobs of the 21st century."

But a ladder to where? That is, where are educated young Americans likely to find good jobs that will not be shipped off to India or China?

The answer, according to a growing number of universities, corporations and government agencies, is in what is being called "services science." The hybrid field seeks to use technology, management, mathematics and engineering expertise to improve the performance of service businesses like transportation, retailing and health care—as well as service functions like marketing, design and customer service that are also crucial in manufacturing industries.

A couple of dozen universities—including the University of California, Berkeley; Arizona State; Stanford; North Carolina State; Rensselaer Polytechnic Institute; and Georgia Tech—are experimenting with courses or research programs in the field.

The push for services science is partly a game of catch-up—a belated recognition that services now employ more than 75 percent of American workers and that education, research and policy should reflect the shift. "Services is a drastically understudied field," said Matthew Realff, director of a new program at the National Science Foundation to finance university research in the field. "We need a revolution in services."

Kurt Koester, a 24-year-old graduate student in engineering at Berkeley, is eager to take part. Yet engineering alone, he observes, can often be outsourced to lower-cost economies overseas.

Mr. Koester's special interest is biomedical engineering, which combines engineering and biology. He is also taking the services science course at the Haas School of Business at Berkeley. He figures it will someday help him manage teams of technologists, spot innovations and new markets, and blend products and services.

"I love engineering, but I want a much broader and more diverse background," he said. "Hopefully, that will be my competitive advantage."

His personal strategy, according to economists, is the best way to prepare for an increasingly global labor market.

"This is how you address the global challenge," said Jerry Sheehan, a senior economist at the Organization for Economic Cooperation and Development. "You have to move up to do more complex, higher-value work."

Representatives from several technology companies, including I.B.M., Accenture, Electronic Data Systems and Hewlett-Packard, and a few universities and government agencies met in Washington in December to discuss how to raise interest in services science.

A further step is a conference on education in services science being held at the National Academy of Sciences today.

Whether services science will ever become a full-fledged academic discipline with departments of its own is uncertain. So far it mainly consists of graduate-level courses and research by professors, though Berkeley will begin a certificate program in the field this fall for graduate students in the schools of engineering, business and information and management systems.

The melding of fields in services science is sure to be tricky. Scientists and engineers tend to regard what is taught in business schools as a mushy combination of anecdotes, success stories and platitudes, wrapped in jargon. Put a few success stories together, and they become a "best practice."

Yet a similar skepticism greeted computing decades ago. When some advocates started promoting the idea of "computer science," traditionalists sneered that any course of study that had to add the term "science" to its name was not a science.

Eventually, computing won over the skeptics. And today, computer science departments are academic fixtures.

I.B.M. was an early champion of computer science, and it is now a leading corporate proponent of services science, sponsoring workshops, awarding research grants and helping develop course materials.

I.B.M. itself is a striking example of the shift toward services over the last decade or two. Once known as a computer maker, the company now gets half its revenue from services. And increasingly, I.B.M. is moving into sophisticated technology services, by working with corporate customers to automate and streamline business tasks like purchasing, human relations and customer relations programs.

In recent years, I.B.M. has shopped the global labor market, expanding significantly in India, especially for software programming work. But it has also reoriented and retrained its existing work force to support the swing to services.

The researchers in its laboratories were dubious at first. "The response here was there is no science in services," recalled Paul M. Horn, the senior vice president in charge of the I.B.M. labs. "But as people got into it, they got excited by working on the fascinating problems in services."

Baruch Schieber, 48, is one of the converts. After joining I.B.M. in 1987, Mr. Schieber did basic research and published articles in scholarly journals, mostly on algorithms that optimize computing calculations. Yet the math techniques used to make work flow efficiently through a computer—a complex system—can be applied to other complex systems in business. That is what Mr. Schieber did, first in manufacturing and later in services.

One recent assignment had Mr. Schieber studying drivers and dispatchers at Boston Coach, a limousine service that operates in 10 cities. His job was to create a computerized optimization system to make sure the company's vehicles and drivers in Boston and New York, where the company handles more than 1,000 rides a day, were used as much as possible.

The system gathered real-time data on car locations, reservations, travel times, traffic patterns, airport conditions and flight times, and it generated recommendations to the dispatchers about which car and driver to send for each ride. As a result, the amount of time the cars had passengers rose 20 percent, and revenue increased 10 percent.

Today, Mr. Schieber is working on a project for the National Wildfire Coordinating Group, a team with representatives from five federal agencies including the Forest Service. His task is to use computer models to help determine where to station limited manpower and equipment around the country to minimize the destruction from forest fires. His models use data on terrain, vegetation, wind, rainfall, public records of fires, and other variables.

Across the spectrum of services, Mr. Schieber sees plenty of opportunity to apply his skills. "There's just so much room for optimization," he observed.

nies, among them national retailers like Sears, and new kinds of industrial organization, like assembly-line mass production.

He points to projects his company is doing as examples of services made possible by new technology. In transportation, networked sensors and analytic software are being used to diagnose the condition of engines. The goal is to make the mechanical upkeep of vehicles like jets and municipal buses more intelligent, shifting from regimented maintenance schedules to as-needed maintenance, which can reduce repair and maintenance costs by 50 percent, he said.

In health care, Mr. Gershman said, it should be possible to use tiny implants to monitor a person's biological functions, whisk reports wirelessly to personalized databases, automatically analyze the results and send alerts and updates to patients and doctors.

"This is how you address the global challenge. You have to move up to do more complex, higher-value work."

The service sector, to be sure, is huge and diverse. There are lots of service workers in low-wage jobs, from fast-food servers to janitors. Services science will have scant effect on them. Their incomes are limited by their lack of marketable skills, not by global competition. Those kinds of local service jobs are not migrating offshore.

An accumulation of technological advances is behind the growing interest in services science. High-speed Internet access, low-cost computing, wireless networks, electronic sensors and ever-smarter software are the tools for building a "globalized services economy," said Anatole Gershman, director of research at Accenture Technology Labs. "That's what is new here."

The current wave of technology, according to Mr. Gershman, is the digital equivalent of national railways and electric motors in the 19th century. They paved the way for new compa-

"Just what will be done with this technology we don't know," Mr. Gershman said. "But the significant thing is that we now have the underpinnings for the construction of new services."

Traditional service functions like marketing and customer service are also being transformed by information technology. The rapid growth of the Web and e-commerce has brought an explosion in the quantity of customer and market data, and a computerized means for tracking consumer behavior.

Today, marketing researchers routinely use analytic and modeling software tools to test hypotheses against statistics from customer databases, polling, economics and sociological studies. "It's really made the field much more scientific," said Mary Jo Bitner, academic director of the Center for Services Leadership at Arizona State University.

Even in manufacturing, the competitive edge of many American companies lies in the intangible realm of service work. Look at the iPod. Apple Computer farms out the manufacturing of its popular music player to subcontractors in Asia. But Apple designed the iPod and wrote the software for easily finding, storing and playing music. It built the iPod brand, and guided its advertising and marketing. In short, Apple keeps for itself the most intellectually challenging, creative work, which adds the most value and pays the highest wages.

The high-end work, experts say, typically taps several disciplines and requires conceptual thinking and pattern recognition. Such work cannot be easily reduced to a simple step-by-step recipe. "Those are the jobs that are very hard to automate or ship to India," said Frank Levy, a labor economist at the Massachusetts Institute of Technology.

Services science is an attempt to give university students a broader set of skills and adopt a broader research agenda for the economy of the future. "We in academia have to find ways to contribute research to improving our economic performance in services and to help students succeed in this knowledge-based services economy," said Henry Chesbrough, who is teaching the services science course at Berkeley.

Letter from Sweden: An Economy with Safety Features, Sort of Like a Volvo

By Alan Cowell
May 10, 2006
(Correction Appended)

When people talk of "the Nordic model" as Europe's panacea they may consider places like this ferry port in southern Sweden, where the Baltic wind lofts the sigh of seagulls over a stilled and silent Ericsson plant.

The factory closed last year after years of job cuts as the telecommunications company reduced its global work force of 107,000 to about 63,000. But for people like Marie-Louise Nordstrom, 53, who lost her position as a purchaser after 35 years in the same factory, the change has been relatively painless.

Under a deal between bosses and labor unions, she and some of the 450 other workers who switched off the lights in December will remain on full pay for 12 months, she said. Then she will qualify for unemployment benefits worth 80 percent of her salary. In the meantime, a private company sponsored by Swedish employers is helping her retrain and recover from the shock of losing her job. "I have learned to be self-confident," she said. "I am not worthless."

At a time when major nations in Continental Europe—France and Italy in particular—are questing in vain for release from the economic doldrums, Mrs. Nordstrom's confidence does not seem misplaced.

The Swedish economy is set to grow by 3.7 percent this year—almost twice the rate forecast even for Germany, the only one of the big Continental European economies showing signs of confidence. Unemployment, though higher than the Social Democratic government admits, is still lower than the nearly double-digit joblessness of France or Germany.

Yet, defying conservative American beliefs, the economy prospers—even though taxes here remain high and big government administers cradle-to-grave

is: Would it work farther south, in Germany or France, or even Italy?

The roots of Sweden's current prosperity lie in the early 1990's when the Scandinavian nations were buffeted by recessions that sent unemployment and budget deficits soaring.

In response, businesses from telecommunications to airlines to banking were deregulated and sold on the open market. State spending was capped, and the budget moved to surplus. Labor laws, which still protect full-time workers, were modified to permit temporary work. The state pension system was overhauled, adding private accounts and encouraging workers

"Our job is to create a society where people are protected and suffer as little as possible and get new chances in society with education and training."

social programs that absorb more than half of the national output.

It is called the Nordic model. The question some Europeans are asking

to postpone retirement in return for higher pensions.

Technology and service companies flourished even as manufacturing jobs were lost. Labor unions, said Ingemar Goransson, a blue-collar union negotiator, saw their mission as "not trying to save jobs."

"Our job is to create a society where people are protected and suffer as little as possible and get new chances in society with education and training," Mr. Goransson said. "There's a social charter, a social contract. There's a general peace contract in Sweden. There's a general culture of problem-solving instead of fighting."

Indeed, as in purchasing their home-grown Volvos, Swedes are prepared to pay top dollar for the safety features: income taxes peak at 55 percent. Traditionally, too, Sweden and other Scandinavian lands have drawn economic benefit from policies that bring women into the work force far more than in some other European countries.

But there was another element that distinguished them from Continental Europe, where globalization is seen as little more than code for the imposition of American slash-and-burn capitalism and the destruction of the welfare state.

"I think the fundamental aspect of the Scandinavian model is trust" among the unions, the government and the people, said Joakim Palme, a leading expert on Nordic welfare systems and the son of the murdered prime minister, Olof Palme. While many in France or Germany fear globalization, he said, "the Scandinavian experience has been to be positive to this change, because it is producing more wealth in the end."

That might be precisely why the Nordic model will not easily take root elsewhere in Europe, as recent street demonstrations against a new labor law showed in France. The question, too, is whether the Nordic model itself can survive at a time when the region, like the rest of Europe, is challenged by immigration, reshaping the social fabric that once hastened reform.

"Sweden is a small country," Mr. Goransson said. "Up to 10 years ago it was very homogeneous as a country. Everything was very alike. Up until then all Swedes looked the same; almost thought the same. Because we are all so equal, we can share the pain of the problems."

These days, though, an estimated 13 percent of Sweden's nine million people were born outside the country, and unemployment among immigrants is significantly higher than among native Swedes. "As Sweden gets more divided, it's more difficult to keep this idea of sharing the pain," Mr. Goransson said.

A report last year by the European Policy Center, a research institute in Brussels, said Scandinavia's "negative approach towards immigration" might "represent the biggest threat to the long-term survival" of the Nordic model, since Scandinavian economies need "a constant flux of foreign talent and workers in general."

Of course, the Nordic model has its quirks.

Sweden's official unemployment rate of 4.8 percent, many economists say, is distorted by the omission of people in government-financed retraining programs. The labor unions calculate the real figure at closer to 8 percent. According to some estimates, Swedes take an average of 17 weeks a year off from work on sick, disability or parental leave, further twisting the statistics. Absenteeism is the highest in the developed world.

And in this debate, size, geography and history do matter. Sweden has been free of war for 200 years. Norway, with 4.6 million people, is rich in oil but fiscally cautious. The economy in Finland, with some 5.2 million people, revolves around the fortunes of the cellphone giant Nokia.

Also, the Nordic countries tend toward the individualism of seafaring lands whose past spanned trade and conquest. Only Finland, the lone republic among the Scandinavian monarchies, joined the euro common currency, and Norway has rejected membership in the European Union altogether.

Compared with some other parts of Europe, there is still some optimism here—at least for people like Mrs. Nordstrom. "I see possibilities, not problems," she said as she surveyed the plant where she worked for 35 years. "I'm glad I have a future."

■ **Correction:** May 12, 2006, Friday. An article on Wednesday about what is known as the Nordic Model for economic well-being referred incorrectly to Finland. While it is among the Nordic countries, it is not part of Scandinavia.

Italy's Once-Plucky Little Factories Now Complicate Its Battle with "Made in China"

By Mark Landler and Ian Fisher
May 14, 2006

To find out why economists have cast Italy as the sick man of Europe, visit this dreary town of little factories huddled in the foothills of the Italian Alps.

Its specialty is brass valves, and in the last decade, the family-owned factories here have watched helplessly as their business has spiraled away, valve by valve, to lower-cost manufacturers in China.

"We don't even know exactly how much of the market we are losing," said

Aldo Bonomi, the general manager of a 105-year-old valve maker founded by his grandfather. "But I am very worried. If I were smart, I'd sell the company before we fall into losses."

Stories like Mr. Bonomi's are familiar in any country that has battled the tide of global competition. What is different in Italy is that the economy—though famous for its supple leather handbags and full-bodied Tuscan wines—depends, to a greater extent than its European neighbors, on mom-and-pop manufacturers that produce everything from valves to mother-of-pearl buttons.

As a result, Italy's economic crisis appears even more intractable than the one faced by Germany, Europe's sick

A miracle of romantic pluck decades ago, the Italian economy has stagnated in three of the six years since the euro existed. Its competitive position has eroded, both globally and in Europe; and its public finances—which Italy cleaned up in the late-1990's to prepare for the euro—have once again deteriorated.

The biggest problem, however, is structural: Italy's thousands of family-owned companies, the secret to its export success in the 70's and 80's, appear ill-suited to the demands of globalization. They make products that can be easily replicated in Asia, using cheaper labor.

"Look at these valves," Mr. Bonomi said, plunking down a matched set.

Nor is Italy's entrepreneurial class likely to take matters into its own hands, as German companies did. Most of the factories are small, and many resist changes like shifting production to lower-cost countries. Italy does not revolve around national identity or M.B.A. theories of good management. The important unit is local, the family, with the equal parts of strengths and messiness that implies.

"These guys really don't want to go," said Roger Abravanel, a senior director at McKinsey & Company in Milan. "For them, to stay at home in Padua or Treviso rather than conquer the world is just fine."

Far from conquering the world, Italy's share of global trade—exports and imports—fell to 2.7 percent last year from 4.6 percent in 1995. Germany's share rose slightly in the same period. In the last five years, German labor costs have fallen by nearly a quarter, relative to Italian costs.

With the adoption of the euro in 1999, Italy's weaknesses became more glaring. For much of the 80's and 90's, Italian governments devalued the lira when they wanted to make their exports cheaper in the world market. Now, Italy has handed over monetary policy to the European Central Bank in Frankfurt, which regards devaluation as a form of voodoo economics.

No other European country has had as fraught a transition to the euro as Italy, which explains why some Italians have come to doubt the experiment altogether. Euroskeptic politicians even demand that Italy abandon the currency and return to the lira.

"Of course we have problems staying with the euro, and that is precisely why we should stay with the euro," said Domenico Siniscalco, a former finance minister in the Berlusconi government who now works for Morgan Stanley. "The euro is forcing virtuous behavior."

Last year, however, Italy's deficit ballooned to 4.1 percent of its gross domestic product, breaching the European Union's deficit cap and rekindling old fears that Italy's untidy finances would jeopardize the euro. Putting the books

Capturing [Italy's] beauty and selling it to the rest of the world is how Italy can reclaim its export franchise and revive its economy.

man for the last several years. While Germany has finally shaken off its malaise, the Italians seem almost paralyzed by their plight—raising fears that their country, lagging further and further behind its neighbors, may loosen the bonds of European integration.

Making a fresh start to catch up with the rest of Europe will not be easy.

Italian voters ousted Prime Minister Silvio Berlusconi last month to a large degree because he did not fix the economy. But then they elected a new center-left government with a parliamentary majority so slim that it may be hobbled before it even takes power.

"I'm not very positive," said Alessandro Profumo, the chief executive of Italy's leading bank, UniCredit. "We have a lot of issues to manage, and the government needs a larger majority to manage these issues."

It is clear why economic fears dominated Italy's recent election, and the epithet "sick man of Europe," conjuring images of the tottering Ottoman Empire, has become shorthand here.

"This one is mine; this one was made in China. It doesn't work as well as mine, but it's close enough."

The Chinese one costs half as much.

Economists offer plenty of remedies for this situation: Italy needs to move into more sophisticated high technology manufacturing. It must bolster its service economy, starting with the tattered tourist trade, which has also lost ground to China. It must shake up its rigid labor market, the main culprit for its high costs.

The trouble is, the incoming government, led by Romano Prodi, does not have the leverage to push for radical change, especially in the Italian Senate, where his coalition holds only a two-seat majority.

"The most likely outcome is that he will water down any reform proposals well in advance to ensure that he faces minimum disruption in Parliament," said Erik Jones, professor of European studies at Johns Hopkins School of Advanced International Studies in Bologna.

in order will be the first challenge for the Prodi government.

Economists speak approvingly of Mr. Prodi's likely appointment of Tommaso Padoa Schioppa, a technocrat and former board member of the European Central Bank, as finance minister.

Any assessment of Mr. Prodi's ability to make other major changes revolves around two poles. The first is his success in pushing through tough changes the last time he was prime minister from 1996 to 1998. The second—the less encouraging side—is his coalition, which critics say is not only dangerously fragile but weighted too heavily toward the far left.

In his first term, Mr. Prodi had the job of preparing Italy to join the European Monetary Union. Then, as now, many experts said the challenge was too great. But Mr. Prodi reduced public debt, made deals with trade unions and imposed a special tax to stem the tide of red ink.

In 1998 a crucial partner, Fausto Bertinotti of the Refounded Commu-nists, withdrew his support and the government fell. Now, Mr. Bertinotti is again in the coalition, this time as president of the Parliament's lower house. Critics say the past could repeat itself, if not with Mr. Bertinotti, then with any of the government's eight other coalition partners.

Allies of Mr. Berlusconi never tire of painting Mr. Prodi's government as a hostage to the left. Mr. Bertinotti and Franco Marini, the president of the Senate, were both trade union leaders. Giorgio Napolitano is the first former Communist to be elected president of Italy.

Critics note that the government plans to repeal part of an innovative labor law, known as the Biagi law, which makes it easier for companies to hire workers on a temporary basis. Advisers to the government insist that any changes will not hinder Italy's competitiveness.

Not everyone is pessimistic about Italy's future. Emanuele Bertoli, the owner of a company that makes mother-of-pearl buttons for clothing designers like Giorgio Armani and Stefano Ricci, has thrived by putting most of his production in Vietnam and China, near the hatcheries for his pearls.

Back home, where he keeps a design studio, Mr. Bertoli, 38, said he was inspired by the sun-dappled landscape east of Milan—a region known as button valley for its many local button makers. "You are surrounded by beauty in this country," he said. "It permeates you."

Capturing this beauty, he said, and selling it to the rest of the world—whether in the form of Ferragamo shoes or Fiat cars—is how Italy can reclaim its export franchise and revive its economy.

"Men and women in the year 3000 will be buying clothes and furniture," said Pier Luigi Bersani, a top economic adviser to Mr. Prodi, arguing that Europe is impossible without Italy. "We have to do better the things that we are already doing."

NOTES